THOMAS VOZZO

CEO OF HOMEBOY INDUSTRIES

THE HOMEBOY WAY

A Radical Approach to Business and Life

FOREWORD BY *NEW YORK TIMES* BESTSELLING AUTHOR
GREGORY BOYLE

LOYOLA PRESS.
Chicago

LOYOLA PRESS.

www.loyolapress.com

Cover art: hand lettering by Fabian Debora, grunge texture, Xurzon/iStockphoto/Getty Images
Back cover, author photo: Eddie Ruvalcaba

Names have been changed to protect the privacy of the people mentioned in this book.

100% of author royalties go to support the mission of Homeboy Industries.

ISBN: 978-0-8294-5456-7
Library of Congress Control Number: 2021947920

Printed in the United States of America.
21 22 23 24 25 26 27 28 29 30 31 Lake Book 10 9 8 7 6 5 4 3 2 1

To my father, who taught us the value of honesty and integrity, and to my mother, who always believed in us—they were truly loving parents.

CONTENTS

FOREWORD

by Gregory Boyle, SJ, founder of Homeboy Industries

I was on a Zoom call with a group in Dublin recently when the host of the meeting quoted an old Irish saying I had never heard before: "It is in the shelter of each other that people live."

This saying captures the essence of Homeboy Industries.

If a prison is how society practices exclusion, then Homeboy Industries practices inclusion. Homeboy Industries is the largest gang intervention, rehab, and re-entry program in the world. It's been around since 1988, and many thousands of gang members have found shelter in the place and each other's hearts. Homeboy Industries puts forward the idea that we need to build a system of care that offsets our over-built system of punishment.

Our CEO for these many years, Tom Vozzo, whose text you now hold in your hands, provides here his "eye-witness" account of Homeboy's counter-intuitive way of proceeding. Before joining Homeboy, Tom had begun experiencing a disconnect between his values and those of corporate America. He soon discovered that there existed two Americas and that, indeed, the poor had been forgotten by one of them.

This realization formed his path to our place in Los Angeles Chinatown, where he chose to be in the proximity of folks in whose vicinity he'd never been before. Tom offers his spiritual and practical accounting of this experience, presented here with clarity and tender grace. His words offer a window into a reality that is uniquely his own and beneficial to us all. His reverence for the complexity of things and his steadfast admiration for the poor's indomitable spirit grace each page and underscore the power of a beloved community of belonging. Systems change when people do, and people change when they are cherished. This is the Homeboy Way.

More than a handful of times, Tom Vozzo has taken a crew of senior staff, all gang members, now in leadership roles, on very arduous hikes. They spend an entire day climbing to heights unthinkable for these guys who have only known the terror of street violence and who have lost nearly half their lives to prison. One particular Saturday, Tom took them all to ascend Mt. Whitney. A homie named José described it as "Horrible. It was intense, and we were exhausted. It seemed like we'd never get there. We stopped talking to each other, much less looking at each other. Everyone had their heads down—just tryna make it. It was all kinda 'every man for himself.'" José told me that many of the homies just wanted to give up and descend the mountain before reaching the pinnacle.

He also shared that Tom noticed the changes that had come over them. At one point, Tom calls them all to attention and proposes the way forward: "You have to look up," he says. "You can't just stare at the ground. Don't forget to admire what you see. Take in the beauty of this place and each other." He invited them to gratitude, which is always bound to happen when we lift our heads. When we stand tall with our eyes open, God becomes recognizable as love, and we realize that community trumps gangs; community trumps the daunting path ahead of us.

Tom and the homies reached the top, and they were thrilled. The tenor of their exhilaration was born from a call to not just put one foot in front of the next. Rather, their joy found its roots in an invitation to look to the sky and to find one's harmonious strength there.

Every morning at Homeboy, we begin the day with "Morning Meeting." We celebrate people's birthdays, sober dates, new jobs, and children being returned to our folks. We announce the tattoo removal hours, give a rundown of classes that day, declare the bread special from the bakery, and finally, we end with the "Thought for the Day."

On one particular day, Tom gave the "Thought." He had finished reading Dorothy Day's autobiography, *The Long Loneliness*. He quoted the founder of the Catholic Worker movement: "I longed for a church near at hand where I could go and lift up my soul." Tom spoke movingly of Homeboy as the place where he palpably feels his soul being lifted up. He has allowed himself to be reached by those on the margins, and the experience has altered his heart.

I am eternally grateful to Tom Vozzo for his singular leadership at Homeboy Industries. He has shown us his humble example of how we are meant to receive people whose burdens are more than they can bear and whose dignity has been denied. He has shown, in this book, a way forward and the path for us all to "look up" and see each other. This book points the way to our foundational joy in choosing to be a shelter for each other and to seek to live in each other's hearts.

PROLOGUE

After working twenty-six years in the for-profit capital sector of our economy, and now after nine years of working with the poor, forgotten, and demonized people of our society, I see life much differently. I feel as if I've awakened to a new understanding of the "societal contract": the rules of how we interact for the betterment of society. The Homeboy Way is the "how" of mutuality, compassion, and kinship, leading to a better society.

I wrote this book because I feel fortunate to have learned so much during my time at Homeboy Industries. To put this in context: I had viewed my life by traditional measures, as being pretty successful and gaining a certain level of stature for what I accomplished. With heightened status comes the usual amount of confidence and sureness about the profound issues of life. And yet through my time at Homeboy, I've come to learn that I didn't know as much about life as I thought. This blind spot I had is typical for so many of us. Through no fault of our own, by just being in the mainstream of society, we stay isolated from those most unlike ourselves and outside our station in life. Without having to come face to face with the marginalized or demonized members of society, we do not have to face the reasons for their circumstances, and we end up being absolutely confident in our view of them and their issues.

Homeboy Industries is the largest and most successful gang re-entry program in the world. It was founded and is led by Father Greg Boyle, a Jesuit priest, who has dedicated his life to helping men and women get out of the gang lifestyle. As they transform their lives, these men and women show us why people should not be defined by the worst thing they've done. Homeboy has helped thousands of people heal from complex trauma and become contributing members of our society. Homeboy helps the people everyone else in society has given up on.

Homeboy Industries is a model program with proven results. It's a special place that offers forgiveness, hope, and "first" chances. And, for so many people, it has become a sanctuary, for it's one of the few places on earth where God is so very apparent.

I arrived at Homeboy exactly when they needed somebody like me with the skill set of running successful organizations. I also arrived at a time when I needed to learn more about myself and my spiritual trajectory. Along the way of helping Homeboy thrive over the past several years, I have gained knowledge and insight about my own spirituality and about the plight of the people Homeboy Industries serves.

I've made friendships and relationships that are remarkable. I've experienced more sorrow and more joy in these past few years than in my whole life before that. I know I'm but a bit player in this story, but my role is that of bringing "privileged eyes" to the message.

I view myself as a reporter to what I saw and as an eyewitness to understanding humanity in a much different way. Along the way, almost by providence, I was able to see how business can be done with a different set of priorities so that everyone benefits: the owners, the management, and those who have never been able to sustain a job but now do. I learned how to help the "unemployable become employable." I participated in the development of business models that provide not just economic impact but social impact. Doing business the Homeboy way is the direction we need to take our collective efforts and is a road map to re-organize the capital markets.

From my first day at Homeboy, I had my head turned every which way as to how Father Greg and the team approach the life challenges the homies faced. Homeboy's approach to helping people was so counter to conventional wisdom that it really caused me to do a double take. And many times, I paused so that I could listen and learn. Fr. Greg's approach was so pure in helping people that I would be cheering inwardly and thinking, *Yes, that's right.* After many years of accumulating these observations, I decided to write this book.

My goal is to share these learnings with as many people as possible in the hope that society at large becomes more aware, enlightened, and compassionate. By breaking the rules of our long-held assumptions, we can finally get to a better place in helping those less fortunate.

In today's environment, we have massive tidal currents flowing around the issues of social injustice and racial inequities. What I didn't know at the time, but do now, is that I was fortunate to be on the front lines with the people involved. This is a story about how a "corporate executive" type became not just a nonprofit CEO of a human-services agency but, more important, a participant in the fight to bring resources and help to those on the margins of our society. Along the way I learned the deep struggles of those less fortunate than me and how the rules of society are stacked against them. I also witnessed firsthand how leaders from the business community, government agencies, law enforcement, justice departments, and elected government stay within their comfort zones and thus perpetuate systems that don't enable true restorative care. I believe the Homeboy way is an antidote to this.

I stand in awe at the resilience of the Homeboy clients. The burdens they carry and the way they move their lives forward is inspiring. From them I have learned to open my heart and be touched by their gentle and authentic friendship. How they understand God's grace has led me to seek my own spiritual journey—the kind of journey we all can take.

I sometimes view this writing effort as writing a love letter to Homeboy. Over the years, Homeboy has had a lot of visitors, and nearly everyone who visits comes away feeling uplifted. I've tried to capture some of that feeling on these pages, to bring the Homeboy culture alive to the reader. It's my life's honor to be a part of the Homeboy community and to serve humbly alongside my fellow humans. I ask that, as you read these pages, you read them with an open heart and fresh eyes. For when we all buy into the Homeboy Way, a movement will be created.

CHAPTER 1

TYRANNY OF THE PENNIES: FROM CORPORATE AMERICA TO A NEW CALLING

The seminal moment of my professional career arrived on a cold and wet Christmas Eve in 2008 while my wife and I were visiting her family in Philadelphia. The nation was amid one of its worst financial crises in history, and the Great Recession was looming. Families were losing their homes, and people stood helpless as they watched their financial portfolios take a nosedive. (We now know that the loss to consumers would eventually equate to trillions of dollars.) Meanwhile, Wall Street and private investors were doing all they could to preserve their financial interests and, by all accounts, still managing to make a killing.

At the time, I was the executive vice president of Aramark and president of Aramark Uniform and Career Apparel Group, then a thirteen-billion-dollar corporation with more than 250,000 employees worldwide. We were profitable, with tremendous cash flow, yet beholden to the "opinions from the street." In the previous year, Aramark had completed a merger with an investor group, creating a private equity structure in which I and 250 other senior Aramark managers were also investors. As it was our first year under private equity, we needed to make sure we hit our financial forecast. All business leaders at that time were trying to get a handle on how the recession would affect business, and it was no different for me at Aramark. As unemployment began to spike from 5 to 10 percent during this period,[1] our sales and services were dramatically reduced because we provided uniforms to people who worked at companies. The fewer people working, the fewer uniforms were needed. Our revenue dropped almost overnight by about the same percentage as the unemployment rate rose. We, like other businesses, were forced to make decisions as we saw the economy spiraling downward.

By December, in the part of the business I was responsible for, we made the decision to cut our labor force by 10 percent—the same percentage drop in our sales. Our plan for the year projected an operating income of about $240 million and net income of about $150 million. Fast-forward a few months, as the recession began to hit hard, and we were projecting to miss operating income by only about $10 million dollars, or just 4 percent of projection. So, instead of $240 million dollars of operating income, it was now going to be $230 million; and instead of $150 million in net income, it was going to be $140 million. This, I thought—considering that our sales were down $120 million—was a pretty darn good result. It took time to figure out how to cut our labor force in the fairest way possible, and those cuts were implemented shortly thereafter.

It was the custom of our chairman at Aramark to call up all the business unit presidents and "higher ups" the day before Christmas to chat about the business and to wish us a good holiday. Each year, I knew to make myself available this day, to be around my desk and ready for his call. I remember the call on this day like it was yesterday. Anticipating his call but needing to prepare for the evening's celebrations, my wife and I headed out to Genuardi's supermarket to pick up a few grocery items for dinner. He called as I parked the car, so my wife went in to do the shopping while the chairman and I began our conversation. He started by asking how the earnings results were going to play out for the year. I explained the ten-million-dollar miss on our $150 million profit plan. He immediately became more intense, and I was surprised by what I heard next. He said, "That's not good enough. We need to get back to what our plan was." He continued, "We need to cut further and do all we can to make our numbers."

---

1. Evan Cunningham, "Great Recession, Great Recovery? Trends from the Current Population Survey," *Monthly Labor Review*, Abstract, U.S. Bureau of Labor Statistics (April 2018), https://www.bls.gov/opub/mlr/2018/article/great-recession-great-recovery.htm.

As he continued to press the issue, I was thinking that during this great recession, to have missed our $150 million profit goal by only $10 million was a pretty good outcome. The set of companies I was responsible for were still going to make $140 million in profit! For the chairman, that wasn't good enough; he was very concerned about the reputation of the company.

I knew that to find that next ten million dollars, I would need to permanently lay off at least 150 more people. We had to cut the next tier of employees, people who had been with the organization for many years. Up until this point, our company had a culture of taking care of people who were good team players and who had shown loyalty and dedication to the corporation. Also, this next round of cuts was going to go deeper into the pool of employees who might not find another job so easily. My mind quickly flashed to two men who worked in the same office building as I did—one was blind, and the other used a wheelchair. Both men were good, dedicated workers who saw their work colleagues as their family.

I also knew that at the end of the day, delivering this result at the cost of another ten million dollars in cuts wouldn't really make a difference in the "market value" of the corporation. It wouldn't make a difference in the lives of the company's owners. We still had big profits. It all came down to "bragging rights" and a sense of honor—to be able to keep your word about the profit line. Were we really about to ruin more lives just so we could prove that we were the most disciplined, pro-investment business folks out there? That even in the middle of a great recession, we were not going to miss our numbers?

This dialogue reminded me of another conversation with the chairman. Shortly after Aramark went public with an IPO (Initial Public Offering) in 2001, the corporation held an investor conference. During this conference, we put on the "dog and pony show" and told the Wall Street analysts how we were going to perform in the future, backed up with charts, graphs, product demos, market research, and more important, a long track record of success. At the end of the day, when the dozen or so analysts were getting into the car service (after being feted all day), one turned to the chairman and off-handedly said, "I still think your dividend will be $.39 a share and not $.40 a share"—which meant we would miss our quarterly profits by a few million dollars. I thought our chairman was going to spit in the face of this young, nerdy analyst. But instead, he turned to the few of us standing there and used the phrase *Ah, the tyranny of pennies.* He continued, "Now that we are in a public world, decisions will need to be made to manage for the penny, and 'heads will roll' if we don't hit our earnings estimate. Changes will occur just to earn back one more penny a share. These decisions might not be good or healthy decisions, but they will be made." His words and that moment have stuck with me.

Our Christmas Eve call in front of Genuardi's ended with the chairman telling me to get it done, no questions asked. I hung up and sat there thinking about it. This was my seminal moment as I newly realized that my values just didn't line up all the way with the values of a big corporation. My view was more long-term. I knew that I wanted to build a great company, and in a great company you need loyal and dedicated people. You need to be committed to your people in good times and in bad. You can't just cut and run on them when times get a little tough. This was the worst economic recession in United States history other than the Great Depression, and we, as a corporation, made a decision that was going to affect our long-term commitment to our employees. I figured there had to be a better way to balance short-term profits against the totality of long-term profits while having the employees of a company remain a top priority.

In that moment, I discovered a yearning to change the rules of the "game," to play a different "game," one in which you didn't exclusively fall back and hide behind "maximize shareholder value." As I write this, I can see people rolling their eyes, seeing me as a hypocrite, thinking, "You're just now figuring this out?" Or, they'll see nothing wrong with maximizing shareholder value. All fair opinions, but for me, none of these opinions matter. What matters is what I do with the knowledge I have going forward.

Business leaders often have blinders on, particularly business leaders who are so far removed from frontline employees that they don't realize the impact of such cost-cutting decisions, particularly those that affect employees long-term. I knew it was my responsibility to follow the chain of command. This was not an issue to resign over. I was not "the owner" of the business. What was being asked of me wasn't illegal or outside the norm. Most other businesses were doing the same thing. Some people think I should have resigned that evening. However, those were the rules of the business world. I aspired to and chose to be in that business world, so I was going to follow those rules. Besides, I also wanted to stay on to make sure that whatever actions we did take had my influence; I felt the responsibility to lead the organization through and out of the recession.

However, a seed was planted in my mind that evening. To find a better way to do business. There, back in 2008, on a wet, rainy Christmas Eve, I knew I wanted to work on a different long-term plan and find a way to run businesses that are successful while standing with their employees. I knew deep down that my values didn't exactly square with the situation and the existing paradigm of corporate America. I needed to change my long-term plan, and the only way to do it was to be in charge of my destiny. I knew that with the right business model, I could achieve this vision. I could perform in the marketplace and do right by all the employees.

The Making of the Six-Million-Dollar Man ($6MDM)

I grew up in a middle-class Italian-American family in New Jersey, with hard-working and loving parents, two brothers, and a sister. We had a very stable upbringing and were given a solid moral foundation and a strong set of values. Sundays, after we attended church, we had a big family meal together. During the week, each of us was expected to get all our chores and homework done before we were allowed free time to spend as we wished. I probably watched more TV than all my other siblings combined. I was enamored with sci-fi and shows where the good guy nabbed the bad guy in the end.

During my teens, *The Six Million Dollar Man* was one of my favorite TV shows. For those of you too young to remember, the premise was this: A "valuable asset," an astronaut, badly injured in a plane crash, was put back together with the most sophisticated technology that six million dollars could buy. He had been transformed. He could run faster, see better, last longer, and was stronger than everyone else. A man-made modern superhero. After 99 episodes, Lee Majors left me with an intriguing thought: can modern technology really make a man better, could that really be true?

My brothers and I were the first generation of my family to go to college. I loved mathematics and was mentored by a brilliant professor while an undergraduate. He showed me how mathematics could be used in the "real world," particularly in business-operations research. His influence led me to earn an advanced degree in mathematical science/engineering from the Johns Hopkins University. Upon graduation I interviewed at various places and received job offers from a wide range of organizations such as American Airlines, the National Security Agency, and RCA.

While a job offer from any of these organizations was the goal of my peers at the time, I was super-intrigued to start with a small business where I could have an impact right away and be immersed in the entrepreneurial spirit. So, when a little family-owned catalog company in Boston came a-knocking, it seemed like the obvious choice. My main job at the beginning was to figure out who to mail the catalog to, which, for a math major, was beyond great. I used statistics to analyze which marketing tactics yielded the highest response rate and made recommendations, based on my findings, as to where best to invest our marketing resources. Over the course of seven years, the company's revenue grew from $50 million to $350 million and was sold for a hefty price to the multibillion-dollar corporation Aramark. I felt good that my work had helped the company become a leader in the industry and a sought-after prize. By all accounts, my time at this once-small, family-owned company was a huge success, and I felt a great sense of accomplishment.

However, this business was not just any family-run business but a New England family-run business. Part of their culture was extreme cost-control. For example, every few weeks they would go around the building and search through everyone's desk looking for extra pencils and pens. You were allowed only one of each. Their cost structure also mandated a layoff of the bottom 10 to 20 percent of workers every January. (They were a seasonal business, and about 40 percent of the revenue came in the last two months of the year.) In addition, all business interactions with outside suppliers were a zero-sum game. We always had to make sure we won the negotiation and that the other guy didn't make money on the deal. Our growth and purchasing power were paramount, and suppliers were forced to take the business for zero profit.

Interestingly, we never really questioned the pressure to hold costs down to this extreme. We knew we were not the owners and that they had every right to make those decisions. And when the business was sold, we never saw the owners again. Not to say goodbye or to hear from them a thank-you for making the business successful, and definitely not to share the wealth. The impact of their legacy on morale was simply devastating.

I took away three main lessons from my time there. First, although cost structure is incredibly important to achieve profitability, it is not right to achieve it at the expense of the workers, particularly as a practice of layoffs during the holiday season to set up the next fiscal year. Second, purchasing power is critical for business growth, but a zero-sum game that causes small suppliers to struggle or even go out of business is not a winning strategy. Last, no one builds a successful and profitable business all by themselves, and the team who helps make it happen should be rewarded, at the very least with the dignity of a sincere acknowledgment. Going forward, I was determined to achieve healthy company culture while growing successful and profitable companies.

The second phase of my career began with a corporate move to Lexington, Kentucky, to assume the leadership role of Galls Inc., the other small family business Aramark had just purchased. I was to work under the previous owner for six months, at which time he would retire and I would officially take over. Alan Bloomfield was a terrific businessman, mentor, and a real merchant. He had an eye for products and knew what would sell. During my first week on the job, he called me into his office late one afternoon. He poured himself a tumbler full of whiskey and sat back to give me advice. He said, "I don't know what they teach you Yankee corporate guys, but here in Kentucky, we do things differently. We run this place like the employees are our children, and I make all the decisions, like I'm the parent. It's sort of like a dictatorship." I would say that Alan was a very benevolent dictator.

Clearly, his opening advice to me was from the perspective of an insider to an outsider, to a Northerner and "corporate guy" as he saw it, so that I understood quickly where I stood in the organization. After about three months, he invited me into his office for another conversation and poured himself another tumbler of whiskey. He asked me if I was ready to take over yet, for he wanted to retire. I knew I was ready. I knew the business well, the team had responded positively to me, but I had the desire to keep Alan on board as a consultant as long as I could get him to stay. He was a legend in the industry and a beloved founder of the business.

For the next few years, we had a terrific relationship, and he taught me so much more about business. In fact, the two main lessons I took away from him were, first, take care of the employees and, second, make sure you have a win-win relationship with your suppliers. If you maintain these two tenets, then the business will be successful. And succeed we did. We grew the business from $70 million to $220 million in seven years. The employees did well, and the suppliers did well, all of which made the corporate culture strong and enduring.

I love to tell the following story about those years, as it highlights the differences between the management teams of these first two family-owned businesses I was a part of. During the eleven years at the first company, in Boston, we had many management retreats. They were all mostly work and just a little bit of fun. In the evenings, we bonded over the challenges of surviving the company culture and the rough justice dispensed by the owners and talked about how to change it. By contrast, during the first few months at Galls, I ran direct reports meetings during which Alan would just sit there and open the mail. On one occasion, I told the team I would like to plan a management retreat and that they should come prepared for the next meeting with ideas. Alan interrupted me and said, "Let's do this our way—not much work and mostly have fun together." He then proceeded to go around the room and ask each person, one-by-one, which type of hard liquor they preferred.

At that time, we had eight people on the leadership team. I sat back and thought, *That's eight bottles of liquor for a one-day off-site trip!* Then Alan suggested that we plan the retreat down at his son's house in the "holler"—back-country valley—and begin the morning with a "shoot." He then proceeded to go around the room once more and asked each person how many guns they would be bringing. By the time the question got to me, I had a knot in my stomach. This didn't sound like a good idea. Also, I did not own a weapon. In fact, I had never even shot a gun. So, when it was my turn, I politely demurred. By the time the count was over, we had enough firearms to invade Tennessee!

The guys said they would help teach me how to shoot a weapon. Over the next two weeks they gave me a firearms safety course and assured me that we would not be drinking *and* shooting. The day finally arrived, and we were off at sunrise. We drove about an hour south to the holler and promptly started the meeting. About two hours later, the team (not me) had had enough of the business portion of the meeting, and everybody went off to the shoot. I held back a bit, but eventually they got me over to the target area and gave me a small pistol. That went fine, but then they gave me a .357 magnum with "hot" bullets. That thing almost tore my arm off! The kick from the shot wasn't anything I had expected. After the shoot, we had fried chicken and drinks. What I loved most about Galls was that they put one another first and business second. As Peter Drucker famously said, "Culture eats strategy for breakfast." No truer words have ever been spoken.

A Growing Career

Over the twenty-one years I was with Aramark, from age twenty-eight to forty-nine, they invested more than five hundred thousand dollars in my professional development and leadership training. Each year they held an annual meeting for the corporation's top two hundred leaders, where the best-of-class business school professors and other industry leaders were invited to come in and give lectures. We attended intensive leadership institutes and hired the best consulting firms, such as McKinsey and Company, Boston Consulting Group, and Bain and Company. As Aramark's leaders, we were kept abreast of the latest and most innovative ideas.

As my career progressed and I took on increasingly greater responsibility, the level of the organization's investment in me also increased. I was assigned an executive coach, who was also a licensed psychologist. His specialty was leadership evaluation and development, as well as organizational design. Having a leadership coach was immensely valuable and made a huge difference in my performance and the performance of my team. I was receiving a level of personal development investment that was truly privileged—only Fortune 200 companies could afford to do so. But that was just the start. When I was promoted to executive vice president (we had a CEO [chief executive officer], a CFO [chief financial officer], and four EVPs [executive vice presidents] for the entire thirteen-billion-dollar organization), the other three EVPs and I were sent to St. Louis for two days of intensive testing and evaluations.

We were chosen from among 250,000 other employees for this opportunity. Over the next forty-eight hours, we individually met with a slew of psychologists and psychiatrists and were given a battery of tests to measure our emotional intelligence, IQ, and business intelligence. We were asked about our parents, our spouses, our children, our business points-of-view. All to figure out if we were "fit" to keep on the ladder. As the weekend wrapped up, I was found to be "fit" and was given a tailored leadership development plan. I also felt that I had been taken apart and put back together again, just like the six-million-dollar man. I recall feeling "faster, stronger, smarter"—somehow machine-like—Aramark's new $6MDM apparatus. I felt grateful for their investment and belief in me.

At the same time, I realized I was trained to be their tool, their top-gun pilot, their corporate warrior, their dream-team player. I was proud of myself for having climbed to that position. I was also aware that I was being pushed into the "game" with their rules—I was a star player working for the owners. From the corporate perspective, these types of investments really work out well. In my time at Aramark, my team and I achieved best-in-industry results and produced well over a billion dollars of operating profit for the shareholders (of which I was one). We had the right business model, the right products and services, talented managers, and investment capital to make it all work. There is no doubt that their investment in me to lead made a difference in the results. It was and still is the smartest way to create shareholder value. Find high-potential talent and invest in them so they can transform into $6MDM business leaders who, in turn, create $6MDM business teams.

Leaving Aramark

As the economy recovered, it became evident that it was time to move on. I had been with essentially the same corporation for my entire twenty-six-year career. I had never left the company to pursue a new job; rather, I had always been promoted to a new opportunity from within. I knew that for my career to take the next step, I had to leave Aramark. I also knew in my heart that I really wasn't sure if I wanted that next step up the ladder. To do so, I'd be aggressively playing the game in the arena I was beginning to despise. I found it incredibly difficult to think all this through while fully involved in my high-level job. At the end of 2010, my "golden handcuffs" that the private equity owners had on me were coming off, and I knew this was the time for a transition. But to what?

I was not going to be promoted again at Aramark, for the chairman / CEO had been there for more than twenty-five years and was not going anywhere anytime soon. The decision to leave Aramark was difficult. I felt a responsibility to my team and to all our employees. I had a fierce loyalty to the company that had chosen me and had invested so much in my development. At times, doubt crept in as I passed up other high-level job offers. I'd ask myself if I simply lacked that "killer corporate gene," or was I merely in the process of transcending all that I had been taught, moving toward a higher calling? A place where the mission was both business and people?

With my position as a corporate officer of a thirteen-billion-dollar multi-national corporation came a set of responsibilities that I took seriously. The professional course of action, given my desire to be in a different spot during 2011, was to work out a transition plan. Upon my telegraphing this intent, the corporation stayed true to their "people as a tool" posture and accelerated our separation talks. I left in January 2011. Long gone are the days of retiring with a golden watch. Instead, it's about the "next man up" to hit the quarterly financial target. In their mind, I had been paid handsomely and done well for the business. But when I didn't show commitment going forward, it was just natural to move on. As it turns out, the best professional part of my life was just about to happen, and I was soon to learn how one-dimensional my life had been.

CHAPTER 2

THE MOVE TO HOMEBOY INDUSTRIES

While at Aramark, the senior leadership was encouraged to get involved in our local communities. Being a services business means that all business is local business. Being a stakeholder in the betterment of the community not only helps local businesses but, by extension, everyone in the community. I got to know The Salvation Army (TSA) during our Aramark community days of service. We'd show up at a TSA location with one hundred to two hundred employees and work with them for a day: cleaning, fixing, and refurbishing its buildings and grounds. For a few years in a row, we went to various TSA locations around Los Angeles, listened to program participants' stories, and learned about their needs. Additionally, I got to interact with the leadership of TSA and always came away impressed with their know-how, empathy, and passion to help people. So when I was asked to join the advisory board, it was an easy decision. What I came to discover was an even deeper appreciation for the men and women of TSA, for they dedicate their lives to serving others, to serving the most in need. One of TSA's mottos is "Heart to God and Hand to Man," which for me perfectly encapsulates what the TSA "workers" do. On a few occasions, as I drove home from a board meeting or from visiting a shelter, I wondered what it would be like to totally dedicate my life to helping people. A lot of folks do it, but I wondered what it would be like if *I* did it. In reflection, I find it interesting how these types of thoughts put things into motion before one even realizes it.

Upon hearing that I left Aramark and would not be pursuing corporate life again, a fellow TSA board member asked to meet with me for lunch. He chose to meet at the Homegirl Café, and I found out that he was the chair of Homeboy's board. Viktor and I became friends and discovered that we were kindred spirits in our approach and desire to make a difference with our business experience. During that fateful lunch with Viktor, he explained Homeboy to me and his vision of bringing in business experience to help the organization through some of its challenges. I quickly stepped in to say that I really didn't want to be on another board at this stage in my life, but I was interested to see if I could make a difference by sharing my business experiences. Viktor jumped into action and quickly formulated a way for me to volunteer and, in particular, focus on Homeboy's businesses.

Before saying yes to the volunteer gig, I asked if I could have a meeting with some of the people involved in running Homeboy's businesses. I saw this as a way to learn the extent of the problems as well as a way to figure out if I could really make a difference. A personal factor in committing to a formal role was the commute. I had just come off seven years of either having a long drive to the office or being on the road two weeks a month all around the country. I was worn out and in no way wanted to sign up for another sixty- to ninety-minute commute on a regular basis. That first meeting with the business players made me hesitate, for what I saw and heard was a lot of infighting, no apparent appreciation of the business skill sets needed, a lack of vision as to where the businesses were headed, and people giving off vibes that they didn't need help. In fact, I called Viktor to talk more about it and to share my concerns. He was persistent and gave me time to think about it. I asked if I could meet with Father Greg before making a final decision. Father Greg Boyle was the Jesuit priest at the helm of Homeboy Industries.

Meeting with Father Greg really turned the decision around for me, for what I came to understand is that the businesses are a vehicle for making transformation happen. Although the businesses are just one aspect of the entire program, the main business purpose was "not to hire homies to bake bread, but to bake bread to hire homies." To bake bread so that we can hire more homies. To hire more homies. This is what appealed to me, to do well in business so that you can hire more people, to give more people a chance to improve their lives.

Father Greg also made it clear that he was open to change for the businesses. In our first meeting, he said we would do what I thought needed to be done. Being a for-profit guy, I'd never dream of inquiring about the program side of the organization, nor did I understand the interplay between the businesses and the programs. I was content to focus on the businesses. But I sensed there was something between the two. I called Viktor up and said, "I'm in to volunteer," but I had two requirements. The first was that even though I'm a volunteer, the business managers needed to report to me. Second, I needed to have a seat at the table where the organization makes decisions (at this time it was called the council). Viktor and Father Greg conferred, and I officially joined the team.

I had been to Homeboy only three times, and I was to start working there three days per week. On my first day of work, I had quite a bit of trepidation. I had never worked at a place where I was a minority. I didn't speak Spanish and have a terrible ear for languages. I was much, much older than everyone else—except Father Greg—and figured that I didn't have a lot in common with these folks. As I will explain later, those were all my perceptions, my concerns alone. What I would discover is that the Homeboy community is very welcoming. Nearly everybody, trainees and staff, were open and looking for help. The business managers, on the other hand, were a different story—more on that later.

To put this in context: in 2010, two years before I started as a volunteer, Homeboy was on the verge of financial failure. It was running a $2 million annual deficit that was growing rapidly year-over-year. It had just invested $11.3 million into its facilities with little more than $2 million a year in business revenue.[2] Homeboy was on the brink of closing its doors and began massive layoffs. At the time, it employed 350+ homies in its eighteen-month training program and served more than eight thousand homies per year with wraparound services, such as tattoo removal, legal aid, and psychological services. Homeboy was the largest gang-intervention and rehabilitation program in the United States, and the cost of its looming failure would be huge.

---

2. Douglas McGray, "House Of Second Chances," *Fast Company* (April 16, 2012). Retrieved from https://www.fastcompany.com/1826868/house-second-chances.

Los Angeles Mayor Antonio Villaraigosa was interviewed at the time on a local talk-radio show, KPCC (89.3), where he shared that he was "saddened" and "concerned" that Homeboy had to lay off 330 of its 427 employees because of a five-million-dollar shortfall.[3] At the time the mayor's office had an annual budget of $26 million for gang reduction and youth development programs. Although Homeboy had the most successful track record in the nation, its bailout came from private donors and foundations, not local government—a frustration that continues to this day.

The Next Step of Faith

At the end of 2012, Homeboy was finding itself in the same trouble: this eleven-million-dollar nonprofit organization had an operating loss of three million dollars. It was my assessment that Homeboy had unparalleled success, almost magical success, in helping its homies transform their lives. That was undisputable. The opportunity that became obvious was that I could invest my time developing the management team's business and leadership skills so that they and the organization could stabilize to implement Father Greg's vision and meet the board's goal to double, triple, even quadruple the number of homies they might be able to help year-over-year worldwide.

My next leap of faith was a shift from being a volunteer guy who was helping out in the businesses to becoming its Chief Executive Officer. I started as a volunteer in October of 2012. During that time, the organization was going through some financial turmoil, and the Board of Directors wanted Father Greg to make some changes and talked about changing him out. Can you imagine Homeboy Industries without Father Greg Boyle? This is a sign of how bad the situation had become. The board felt pressure to do something and was too far removed from understanding how the organization worked; so they went toward a "defcon 5" action. Fortunately for Homeboy, Gayle Northrop was around as a board-sponsored consultant, and she saw that the

---

3. Dennis Romero, "Mayor Villaraigosa 'Saddened' By Anti-Gang Group Homeboy Industries' Financial Woes," *LA Weekly* (May 14, 2010). Retrieved from www.laweekly.com/mayor-villaraigosa-saddened-by-anti-gang-group-homeboy-industries-financial-woes/.

path forward was not to remove Father Greg Boyle from the organization but to blend professional management into the staff to stabilize the organization.

Without my knowing, Gayle suggested to Greg that perhaps it would be a good idea to ask me to come on as temporary, part-time CEO. They designated the position as part-time because they knew I was only doing part-time work in the businesses and that fit my desired lifestyle. So, in early December, Greg asked me to come to his office and offered me the position as CEO. He did it in his usual no-pressure way, saying "come join the community," "we need you," "you've been good for us," always in a humble and charming sort of way. I was honored to be asked and Gayle had given me some sense that this might occur. So, after a few questions of Father Greg, that mostly had to do with whether he wanted this to happen or if he was merely doing this at the behest of the board, I gave the offer serious consideration. While it's true the board wanted this, I also heard the desire in Greg's voice; in certain ways he was tired of dealing with day-to-day issues and the pressures of running a sizable nonprofit. I then asked him to give me some time to think about it.

So here I was in late 2012, feeling as if everything in my whole life had led me to this moment. The skills I had developed over my twenty-five-year business career and all the investment to make me into the $6MDM were all for the role I am in today: to help and eventually lead one of the most important organizations from financial instability into a bright future, to "bake more bread so we can hire more homies." To develop homies into successful leaders who will run Homeboy long into the future.

When this opportunity presented itself, I was cocksure of my business and leadership skills. I figured it would be easy and thought maybe I'd learn something from Father Greg. Most important, I saw this as an opportunity to give back—which was a strong driver for me. I saw myself as a "consultant": I would impart my knowledge, straighten out Homeboy's social enterprises, exit after a short period of time, and then figure out the rest of my professional life.

My conversations with the staff about taking on the CEO role went, overall, fairly well. The consistent feedback I received is that Homeboy had been through a number of "professional manager" types and it didn't end well for the organization nor the executive. As I delved into this further, I came to learn that the other professionals Greg has depended on either were not good at the job, never really understood the mission, or thought they knew better than Greg—and let everyone know about it. In the end, the organization rejected these folks and hence were circumspect about another guy coming in for the same result and yet they knew it was needed.

Talking to my wife about joining Homeboy was a bit more challenging. After a twenty-six-year corporate executive career, I had committed to not working full time again and traveling quite as much. Here I was now, thinking about signing up for a full-time gig and taking on the pressures of running another organization. On top of that, she had not yet visited Homeboy, so she really didn't understand the program and the draw it had for me. As always, most of these concerns were my own projection. She fully supported my decision and had noticed in the few short months of my volunteer time how excited and motivated I was to be at Homeboy.

While volunteering at Homeboy for a few days a week, I was also pursuing another goal in a private equity firm. This would have meant a big investment and responsibility as a board member. Eventually, I found myself in a position where I had to make a choice . . . Make a lot of money for myself or become CEO of Homeboy.

If I took on this role of running a nonprofit organization, I was concerned about how the business world would view me, so I made some calls, talked to professional recruiters, etc. Most people confirmed my suspicions. If I took this job, within a year's time, I'd be unhireable somewhere else. Big business would think I was out of touch.

Did faith play a part in my decision? I believe so. It was faith, not in the spiritual sense, but the faith in taking a step in a direction that felt like taking a step in the dark, but feeling comforted that it would be okay. Logic didn't lead me to being at Homeboy. A certain faith did. For the first time in my professional life, I acted on faith.

I think back now about how that faithful decision turned out to be one of the best decisions I've made in my life. At the time it seemed momentous and risky. But really, I live a "charmed" life, and if Homeboy didn't work out for me, I'd be no worse for it. I've come to realize that for our homies, the faith they have is truly awe inspiring. They often leave everything they have and everybody they know behind so that they can move their life forward. That takes faith.

It's uncomfortable relinquishing yourself to faith. You are not in control and yet you need to have an open heart and mind. You need to push beyond a lifetime of effort to stay in control and in charge. Writer, teacher, and spiritual leader Richard Rohr talks about this kind of faith in this way:

> Not knowing or uncertainty is a kind of darkness that many people find unbearable. Those who demand certitude out of life will insist on it even if it doesn't fit the facts. Logic and truth have nothing to do with it. If you require certitude, you will surround yourself with your own conclusions and dismiss or ignore any evidence to the contrary. . . . The very meaning of faith stands in stark contrast to this mindset. We have to live in exquisite, terrible humility before reality. In this space, God gives us a spirit of questioning, a desire for understanding. In some ways it is like learning to "see in the dark." We can't be certain of what's in front of us, but with some time and patience, our eyes adjust, and we can make the next right move.[4]

Faith comes in different ways, and I've learned to have faith in our mission and how it keeps going. My first year at Homeboy was the most stressful professional year of my life, and yet the most exhilarating and formative. The one question this $6MDM didn't ask prior to taking on the job was "How much money do we have in the bank?" Turns out we had very little. Three weeks into my tenure as CEO, the organization was on the brink of collapse. This situation snuck up on the finance team (again professional managers letting Greg down). At that time Homeboy did not have any banking relationships and thus couldn't borrow money, even on a short-term basis. I and another board member loaned the organization money to make payroll to keep everything afloat. From there, Greg and I went out and met a lot of people to raise money for future payrolls. I then put the organization in a downsizing and rightsizing mode. We laid off 15 percent of the staff, reduced everyone's pay, implemented furloughs, I stopped taking a salary (and still don't), and we scaled back on the number of clients we served. All year long, it was a close call in making the

---

4. https://cac.org/waiting-and-unknowing-2019-12-01.

payroll every other week. I knew that if we could get to the end of the year, when our Holiday fundraising was significant, we would make it and I could help the organization avoid closing its doors and the public embarrassment of its failure.

At the beginning of my time at Homeboy, some of the staff often questioned why I joined them. Was it to burnish my reputation and use Homeboy as a stepping stone? Was it to "make amends" for some "bad" thing I did? Was it to "take over" the businesses and make money? Was I here because I felt guilty about the amount of money I had made in my life? The speculation was endless and when asked I just honestly said, "I'm simply here to help." I knew I had lived a charmed life and wanted to give back. While this answer is the truth, it really didn't satisfy the questioners.

I struggled to find a deep answer that satisfies people. I'll say that Father Greg never once questioned my motivation nor reasons for being at Homeboy. I now know the answer. I'm at Homeboy to discover more about faith in general, and in particular, *my faith*. While I've always thought of myself as a faithful person, it was always abstract intellectual exercise. I'm now discovering it at a "gut and heart" level. As Richard Rohr writes in his book *The Universal Christ*, "[f]aith at its essential core is accepting that you are accepted." What Homeboy has shown me is that I'm accepted by God—always, and no matter what.

Shortly after Father Greg asked me to come onboard as CEO, I was having a conversation with Hector Verdugo. Hector is the Associate Director of Homeboy Industries. Hector is in charge of all the trainees. He came up as a trainee and up through leadership. Hector is a man with a lot of wisdom, but in many ways he doesn't always give himself credit for it. Early on, as I was sitting there, talking to Hector, trying to understand the organization better, understanding his insights into different trainees and why we help them in such a way, we got to a conversation about my role at Homeboy. I was talking to him about why I thought I was joining Homeboy and how I was here to help. All of a sudden he looks up at me and says, "But you do know Homeboy is going to change you and you're going to learn a lot from Homeboy?" When he said it to me, I said to myself, "That's a nice phrase." I smiled and I said politely, "I hope so." But deep down I didn't think so, "What can I learn from Homeboy? Who's going to teach me, the $6MDM who's been involved in so many other businesses of scale?" Hector gave me that knowing nod back, knowing that while I said yes, I really didn't believe it, and he knew I didn't believe it, but he also knew it to be true.

CHAPTER 3

"CORPORATE GUY" MEETS A DIFFERENT KIND OF ENVIRONMENT

It is not uncommon to feel a bit of sensory overload as you walk through the doors of Homeboy for the first time. Without fail, the space is likely to be bursting at the seams with a mass of people, all milling around and talking. Although the environment is chaotic, it's upbeat, and you feel a good vibe—an energy, a chi, a remarkable feeling of acceptance as you glance around, making eye contact with folks. Often, before you even get through the front door, a guy with a lot of tattoos will greet you and say, "Welcome to Homeboy." Chairs line the left side of the reception area where people—a lot of people—sit and wait to either go to their counseling session, their tattoo-removal appointment, their GED class, or to meet with Father Greg. Intermingled amongst all these past and present gang members—most of whom are Hispanic, Latino, or African American in their early twenties—are "regular" folks, like myself, mostly white or Asian, above the age of forty, who are coming in to volunteer, who have a business appointment, or are there for a tour. The beauty of the open space is that within the atrium's three hundred square feet, you have a melding of the outside world and the inside world, the building of a community between those who "have a lot" and those who are truly poor (not just in the economic sense). It is the space where the line between the "important people" and the "forgotten" of our society begins to fade away.

If you are lucky enough to arrive at Homeboy by eight thirty in the morning, you will experience our morning meeting along with a couple hundred or so other people from our community. Homies take turns kicking off the meeting each day, sincerely welcoming all those who are present, sometimes with nervous or anxious voices—for many, it's the first time they've spoken in front of a large group—and the homies waste no time encouraging their peers. Our mission statement is read next: "Homeboy Industries provides hope, training, and support to formerly gang-involved and previously incarcerated men and women, allowing them to redirect their lives and become contributing members of our community." This ends in loud applause and cheers. Another homie will take the mic next (also likely to be someone very new to public speaking), announcing the class schedule for the day (which elicits an "all damn day!" response from the crowd), other general announcements, and more hoots and hollers for those who've passed their driver's-license test or GED or who've achieved a sobriety anniversary. If it's somebody's birthday, we will sing Happy Birthday to him or her too; for many, this is their first experience of having "Happy Birthday" sung in their honor.

Then Father Greg (when he is not on the road fundraising) or one of our homies or staff will lead a "thought of the day," typically an inspirational message that reflects on a personal experience of transforming pain, loss, or hardship into healing, love, or kinship. I encourage you to google "Homeboy Thought of the Day," if you've never heard one before. The daily devotional ends in a prayer of gratitude to whichever God one wants to pray to. Then, everybody gets to work.

In many ways, our morning meetings are the glue that keeps our healing culture strong. For the clients of Homeboy programs, the stakes are high and the cost of failure incalculable. We know that if our doors fail to open, more than two hundred gang members would be back on the street doing their best to survive. Although the resiliency some have gained through our program might enable them to stay on their new path, the allure of seeking emotional support in old neighborhoods will be too great for others. They will be toppled by challenges most of us can't begin to comprehend, and they'll habituate back into gang life—if they survive at all. The generational cycle of violence and poverty will continue. Homeboy's leadership and governance effort to keep the doors open remains gravely important.

When homies come into our eighteen-month therapeutic program, they enter as trainees and will eventually be placed into one of our social enterprises businesses. However, before work therapy begins, a whole team of talented and dedicated professionals surround them—literally and figuratively—initiating the positive bonds and emotional support that will enable his or her individualized recovery and development plan. Currently, we have only enough resources to select one new trainee each week out of a pool of more than one hundred applicants we might have at any given time. While on average we take in one new person each week, some weeks it's four, other weeks it's eight. This is particularly true when youth camps release young men in large groups at one time. When this happens, we need to go long stretches of time not accepting anyone else because we have exceeded our capacity. How does one go about choosing what for many could mean the difference between life and death? I've been serving on the selection committee and participating in interviews for eight years now. Among my observations is that each and every person who is looking to be in our program has the desire to "do good," "to be better," "to be the person they are meant to be." The struggle is that they don't know how to make this transition on their own.

What I have found so interesting is that when tough gang members come to Homeboy for the first time, in many ways it's more intimidating for them to enter the atrium area than it is for an outsider. Gang members are hesitant to enter a building they know is filled with guys from so many different gangs, and they are conditioned to think that they might get jumped by a rival gang member—just by being there. José, one of our key leaders, tells the story of the first time he walked through our doors:

> When I arrived at Homeboys I looked around and thought, *Damn, there's a lot of gang members here. Maybe this place isn't for me?* I'm sitting in the lobby and I notice Mario, the homie with the most tattoos in the building—he works in the café. Anyway, I notice him notice me, and he begins to walk towards me. As he approaches, my heart races. I'm prepared for the worst. He walks up and says, "Hey, my name's Mario. I've never seen you here before. Do you want something to drink? Some water or something?" I couldn't believe it. A gang member from a different gang asking me if I was thirsty? What a trip.

So, the warmth and friendliness of Mario begins the transformation of José. This is an example of the magic of Homeboy: one homie shows another homie the way, lends him a hand, shares with him, walks with him. Through shared tragedies and a desire to change their lives, a group of men and women help one another along to make a better life for themselves in, as Father Greg says, exquisite mutuality.

Healing and Transformation

Transformation happens at Homeboy, unbelievable transformation in fact. We serve those who are suffering and trying to heal from the severe trauma of their past. Many don't understand that the violent trauma they experienced has left them with unmanageable and ongoing symptoms of C-PTSD (a condition marked by repeated and frequent trauma as opposed to the experience of a single traumatic event).[5][6] This understanding is a key aspect vital to enabling them to begin their transformation. Once this occurs, there is hope that their C-PTSD will become manageable. Part of that transformation process, in our view, is discovering one's self-worth. This is facilitated through many modalities, including one-on-one therapy, group work, life-skills classes, mentorship, rituals, retreats, movement classes, and spirituality. All of that happens at Homeboy in a unique and unassuming way. Many people ask me what makes Homeboy so successful, and I say it's really as simple as our fundamental tenet to practice kinship and compassion. They say, "But your clients are so tough to work with and have had such traumatic pasts. How is that possible?" We nod and share Father Greg's words: "There's no way out of pain other than through it, but here [at Homeboy], you can go through it surrounded by love."

Another aspect of healing from C-PTSD and beginning the process of transformation is helping our homies deal with the emptiness, despair, and brokenness that have set in from years of being demonized, of being told they will never amount to anything, that they are worthless, that they should just

---

5. Matthew Tull, PhD, "What Is Complex PTSD?" *Very Well Mind* (May 4, 2021), www.verywellmind.com/what-is-complex-ptsd-2797491.

6. Seth J. Gillihan, PhD, "21 Common Reactions to Trauma," *Think, Act, Be* in *Psychology Today* (September 7, 2016), https://www.psychologytoday.com/us/blog/think-act-be/201609/21-common-reactions-trauma.

be locked up. Arriving at Homeboy, such emptiness and despair are accompanied by their openness to the possibility that the Homeboy promise of transformation they've seen or heard on the street or in prison might be available to them, too. We simply embrace them, no questions asked. Our tireless mentors, case managers, educators, mental health professionals, and many, many other program facilitators and community leaders get into compassionate kinship with them almost immediately.

Our whole organization's purpose is to provide healing for those who have been traumatized, been broken, been beaten, been forgotten, been sidelined, been marginalized. Healing leads to transformation. We say that a healed individual is a transformed individual. More practically, that healed individuals are resilient individuals, for who among us can deny another human life from feeling protected and safe? It's amazing and awe inspiring that in the course of eighteen months we are able to watch people transform before our very eyes.

I remember being a part of María's selection committee. She was recently released from prison and would not look straight at you. She was a hard-core gang member, tough and stern with her words, anger lurking just below the surface. Yet she had the courage to ask for help, and help is what we gave her. During her time with Homeboy, we all got to witness her open up, heal her wounds, redirect her anger, and prove more than capable of doing a lot of different jobs. By the end of her time with us, her wide smiles were infectious; she was so friendly to so many. María left Homeboy to become a solar panel installer and now gets paid quite well.

I also recall Pablo, a big guy, so big you knew he had been one of the people to watch out for, and yet he knew his persona was a mask. People used him for his intimidating size and put him in situations that were not good. At Homeboy, he learned that we didn't care about all that, that we only wanted to see him succeed in what he wanted to do. He learned to take off that mask, to be comfortable in his own skin, and when he left us had "graduated" to a job that also pays good wages. Or Moisés, an older dude who had a lifetime of addictions and run-ins with the law. He was in and out of our program a few times because he couldn't stay clean, but he eventually got sober and came back into our program. His healing led to an aspiration to enroll in truck-driving school, so we helped him with that. He now has a job driving for a living. There are dozens and dozens, hundreds and hundreds, of these stories of transformation, all truly amazing and awe inspiring.

These transformations are more than I think I would have accomplished had I grown up under similar circumstances. I believe that one reason Homeboy has so many compassionate, generous donors and volunteers is because each of us has a dark emptiness of one kind or another. That perhaps we also feel the pain and joy within ourselves when we see people who have it far worse than we do, "do it." We want to reward the joy we feel when we witness a homie fill his or her emptiness, to be part of it, to emulate it. I often tell our clients that they truly are role models for the rest of our society, but they don't believe me, because all their lives the rest of society has told them otherwise.

New Understandings of Workplace Dynamics

One issue that was a head-turning topic for me as a for-profit business guy coming into the organization was what I perceived to be insubordination within our team, particularly our trainees. To put it in context, about 90 percent of our folks have never worked longer than a month in the formal economy, whether they're getting out of prison at age nineteen or at age forty-nine. They just haven't worked "on the outside" and certainly never had the privilege of being trained. The rest of us in America clearly understand the generally held norms of work ethics. We as outsiders understand the unwritten rules of workplace etiquette, that when your superior tells you something, you get it done. That, in general, you don't question it, talk back, you don't give attitude, and you're not flippant about it. But for all their lives, our men and women have had people in authority tell them to do things, a lot of things they didn't want to do, whether it was at home, in school, on the street, or in prison. To gain compliance, or as punishment for noncompliance, authority figures sent the emotional and physical message, "You're no good." For many of our folks, these punitive incentives and verbal abuse transformed the concept of work into a literal power struggle.

At a morning meeting one day, one of our graduates of the program, Sebastian, was telling a story on this topic to impart wisdom to the newer folks in the program. He talked about the beginning of his time at Homeboy: how much he hated to work, how he thought it was beneath him, how he didn't come to Homeboy to do physical work, that he came to Homeboy so that we could help him with his anger. How, in his early days at Homeboy, he was frustrated with us for making him do manual labor. He led this message at the morning meeting in a typical Sebastian way, with attitude, humor, and humility. He told of a moment early in his time at Homeboy when his supervisor, Edwin, came over to him and said, "Go pick up that trash off the floor near G's office." Sebastian's response? "You saw it first. You pick it up."

It took me some time to understand that insubordination is not what's underneath the surface. It's not that our homies don't want to pick up trash or do the work. The complaints and attitude are not about the work itself; rather, they are about what certain types of work represented to them in their former lives at home, on the street, and/or in prison. "Manual labor" (think of the most awful ways people must use their bodies to survive) was often reserved for the most oppressed in these social structures as a way to strip away their dignity, to reinforce judgments of failure, even to punish with traumatizing effect. At Homeboy, we use work therapy as a means to undo and restore this loss of dignity. Everyone at Homeboy, at one time or another, has swept floors on behalf of the organization. This is hard work, and there's dignity in it. It is in this hard work that profound healing paradoxically begins. I will never look at "insubordination" the same way again.

I came to understand that for the most part, when people engage in backtalk or are insubordinate, it's not about whether they want to be part of our program, and it's not about a lack of desire to do well in work. It's about overcoming the myriad struggles in their lives at that moment in addition to reclaiming dignity at work. They have so many things pressing on them, whether court appointments, debt that's mounted up, a baby mama giving them drama, a custody fight for their kids, mental health problems that need managing. Finally, they are beginning to recognize the issues they had earlier in life, and those memories retraumatize them—while they are doing their Homeboy jobs. Insubordination is not about disbelieving in their supervisor or disrespecting their supervisor. Insubordination is mostly about other things going on in their lives, and we're here to help them move through that.

This is not to excuse the infighting, bad attitudes, and lack of responsibility I witnessed early on at Homeboy. For the most part, these instances were among some of the "outsiders" at Homeboy, those responsible for governing and managing the business side of the organization. Although these individuals did not go through our program, I felt that they *thought* and *cared* about our mission a great deal but struggled to *experience* it in a profound way. Some saw themselves as "above" our clients. Furthermore, their work habits were not of the "leadership by example" ilk but more akin to the trainees who didn't know better. Perhaps there was even some innocent blindness caused by their privilege.

I had thought that my biggest challenge was to "root out" insubordination in general, but it was really to manage through a murky balance. Let the insubordination of the trainees go while holding the management team to a higher level of accountability and professionalism. This insight caused me to manage the team with two perspectives in mind: of those who were in the process of reclaiming dignity at work and of those who were stuck in their own frustrations and resentments.

I'm thankful that my misunderstanding about insubordination and subsequent bad attitudes about it were met with patience and tenderness from Father Greg and the homies. Can you imagine how this type of tenderness and understanding might transform workplaces on the "outside"? I have come full circle in my thinking. While I would take pride in managing everybody equally, I now know that I need to lean in with the trainees and the management teams in different ways. I was careful to make sure I declared this upfront; however, many people became frustrated with me over time. They felt that I favored the trainees who became managers because I did not hold them to the same high accountability standard as I had for everyone else. I am totally comfortable with this approach and believe it needs to be followed more for those organizations looking to develop employees from different lived experiences and economic strata.

Nearly seventy-five years ago, Dorothy Day said, "Every one of us who was attracted to the poor had a sense of guilt, of responsibility, a feeling that in some way we were living on the labor of others. The fact that we were born in a certain environment, were enabled to go to school, were endowed with the ability to compete with others and hold our own, that we had few physical disabilities—all these things marked us as the privileged in a way."[7] When I put on my $6MDM hat and looked at our homies as employees, I began to realize that it was this understanding of the plight of the less fortunate and a desire to make change that had driven me away from Aramark. Little did I know that a healing transformation was occurring in me at Homeboy. One that began with repeated experiences of being filled with grace while I worked, while I did my job. Of being reunited to my nature, from which my job (and training) had previously distanced me.

Laughter and Hugs

In reflection, I see that the elixir that helped me return to myself was the laughter and steady stream of hugs one experiences here. Perhaps they go hand in hand. A community in which so many people offer hugs for friendship and support is the same community in which people are so comfortable with themselves that laughter happens naturally and often. The laughter doesn't come from telling jokes or pulling fast ones on each other (although both do happen). It's more about homies finding humor in life and leaning into that humor. The sly smile, the sparkle in one's eyes, the playful teasing—all of it happens in such an authentic and unbridled way. Most of the laughter comes from enjoying the humility that is found in one's self-deprecating way of being wrong, or out of touch, or unsophisticated. The poor at Homeboy are rich in that "thing" our humanness desires.

Workplaces that you and I are used to have humor and good-natured ribbing, but usually it's confined to the lunchroom, or the beginning of a meeting or at after-hour get-togethers. At Homeboy it's there all day: at the beginning of a meeting, during a meeting, and at the end of the meeting. The attitude of,

---

7. Dorothy Day, *The Long Loneliness* (New York: Harper & Row, 1952), 204.

"Let's not take ourselves too seriously," is there on the surface, which is healthy because it doesn't disrespect the situation but recognizes that none of us is the be-all and end-all. We are participating in life as a community and not as separate individuals. Laughter is a great unifier among our population and a bridge builder from those on the inside of Homeboy to those on the outside (the rest of society). Who among us doesn't laugh? Who doesn't smile at funny stories? Who doesn't find delight in seeing others laugh? It's natural. It's an elixir.

For me, the $6MDM who always had my "corporate hat" on, all buttoned up and straitlaced, the amount of humor and laughter I heard over those first several weeks at Homeboy was quite disconcerting. I had a job to do, and I needed everyone to pay attention. I thought that if they were having fun, then they were not working hard enough. I cringe even as I write these words. How wrong I was. Gradually, during those first few months I relaxed more and joined in the humor and the laughter. I think every time I laughed, more of my $6MDM skin molted away, until finally, I was able to just let it happen, enjoy it, revel in it, and use it to connect with others. The big lesson for me was the obvious one of not taking myself too seriously, that being in community is far better than being known as a "serious man" who was all ego driven.

Hugs were the hardest thing for me during my first several months at Homeboy. We are a hugging culture. I was never in a hugging culture and never wanted to be because I didn't know the rules. Whom do you hug? When do you hug? How do you hug? What's a good hug, what's an offensive hug, and why hug at all? All those thoughts went through my mind at Homeboy. I wanted to fit in, but hugging? I have been well taught through years of human resource department training that it is just safer to avoid physical contact with coworkers, particularly if you are in a position of authority or power. Nevertheless, I began to be a hugger. To this day, I can't read the nonverbal cues as to when a hug is allowed. Others just jump right in, but I still hold back. However, I do say that it feels good to be hugged, and I wish I were more of a natural at it. I've heard our folks explain various ways of hugging. There's the chest-to-chest style, the heart-to-heart style, the side-style, the head-up style, the head-down style. The quick-hug, the long-hug, the tight-hug and the really-tight-bear-hug. The man-to-man is different from the woman-to-woman hug. I've learned that at the heart of hugs, they are really just about people being supportive of each other. For so many of the trainees and staff, it's a show of comfort and security, like what a parent gives a child.

So, as I began to address the business challenges at Homeboy, I was the awkward recipient and giver of a lot of hugs. I sensed it was painfully obvious to most that this $6MDM was struggling to reconcile the many "business norm offenses" observed early on (of which I felt there were many) with the humbling process of discovering and learning to be a complete human being at work.

During this early time, I started to understand that so much of what I had learned about people in the workplace didn't apply to this population. On the outside, workplace culture is typically about monitoring and controlling behavior to avoid negative publicity or lawsuits, so when I saw these workplace "rules" being broken, I silently cheered it on. Breaking the rules made sense.

During these first several months, I began to understand that Homeboy's deeper purpose wasn't even about providing jobs and job training—it was about healing. Everyone in the Homeboy community does whatever it takes to help the individual before them transform their life—and that takes top priority over everything else. It was an eye-opening experience that the individual was more important than the financial health of the organization. This excited my inner sense of right. That voice inside me told me to lean in and learn.

As I was falling in love with Homeboy, I sensed dark times coming. My business instincts were telling me that while the team was hugely successful with the mission, its business model was failing. The organization was under massive financial stress, yet the mission kept going without concern for the future. I knew my job was to become the latest person to attempt to fix the financial instability so that the mission could endure. I foolishly also started to wonder if "healing" and "jobs" could coexist. I would later come to regret these thoughts, but they are typical of an outsider's first view.

My sense of guilt and obligation started to grow, for it felt good to be needed by the organization, but I knew I needed to deliver.

CHAPTER 4

"MARGIN *AND* MISSION" VERSUS "MARGIN *OR* MISSION"

During my first few weeks at Homeboy, I set out to begin an assessment of what was working and what wasn't working within the organization. A critical assessment point was how business decisions were being made. Prior to my coming on board, most of the business decisions were made ad hoc, to the best of the ability of the person or people making the decision in a given situation. Because Homeboy is extremely mission-driven, often business decisions were made from the standpoint of how best to help the client in the short-term as opposed to how best to help the business in the short-term so it can help more clients in the long run. My approach was to listen, ask questions, and first and foremost, try to understand their challenges. What I needed to understand better was how the mission-driven dynamic of running the business supported the agency's training program.

Within the building at Homeboy are three different businesses: the café, the bakery, and the merchandise store. Like everywhere else in the building, there are too many people for the space given, but true to the Homeboy spirit, somehow it all works out. I remember quite distinctly my first weeks of working with these businesses. The merchandise store is about one hundred square feet with stacks and stacks of Homeboy T-shirts, jackets, and coffee mugs. Here we do as the museums do: finish all tours at Homeboy with a stop in the Homeboy gift shop.

The shop, like all our businesses, is managed by a former trainee, and the workers in the store are current trainees. The team does a terrific job of engaging customers as they walk into the shop, sharing Homeboy history and answering questions. There, I first realized that we don't have a "normal" workforce. One of the trainees was a quiet fellow named Amos. He seemed to take my business direction well, and I could tell he was very capable. As time went on, he was given more responsibility and then, one day, a few months into my tenure, he stopped showing up.

For a few days, no one had any idea what happened to him. We came to find out that he had been arrested and sent back to prison. The arrest was over an old issue, not something that had happened since his recent release. So, here I was the newbie; I saw the potential in him, I saw his hard work, positive attitude, and a strong desire to turn his life around—but now he was going back to prison. I learned from the council that going back into prison is a dangerous undertaking and its psychological impact will more than likely mean that Amos will be lost to our society. His time at Homeboy, where he found himself and a passion to want more out of life, now might be extinguished. All for an incident in his past when he was another person—it's so counterproductive and heartbreaking.

My introduction to the Homegirl Café was illuminating as well. The café had mostly a women-only work team, for we've learned that women who have been incarcerated and affected by gangs need their own environment in which to flourish. When visitors ask me about the women in our program, I explain that without a doubt, gang members are the forgotten and demonized people in our society, but the women who are around gangs or—to use the police term—*affiliated* with gangs, are even worse off, for they are often and largely the victims of abuse from the male gang members and become their baby mamas. While the gender split in gangs is roughly 95 percent male to 5 percent female, at Homeboy, about a third of our trainees are women. In the café, there are too many workers by intent. Compared to a for-profit business, there are three times the number of workers because it's a training program. Our goal is to put as many people into work therapy as soon as possible. I had to get used to the notion that not all the workers we have are being productive and constantly busy by "standard business measures." What they are learning is to show up on time, how to take instruction from their supervisors, and how to be courteous to the customers. This socialization process is part of the foundation that allows our homies to feel safe, to be "seen," to feel valued and, ultimately, to find the dignity that for so long has escaped them.

During my first few weeks, the managers took me on a tour of our community gardens and set it up so that I would meet the café's maintenance supervisor, Miriam. Miriam was a homegirl from a local gang and talked often about her battles to change her life and about her goals of becoming a car mechanic. She mentioned being shot in the chest. As I listened to her tell the story, she did it with no extra bravado or remorse, just explaining what happened and expressing her desire to move past all that. This was the first time I realized that within the context of a job at Homeboy, someone has the opportunity to become better than their past, to move beyond the hopelessness of gangs. Without Homeboy, Miriam and folks like her would not have a chance to transform their lives.

Homeboy Bakery is the business with the greatest number of trainees because nearly all the breads, pastries, and desserts are handmade. I love to start my day by walking through the bakery and observing the team in action. The smells are just heavenly, but for me, a guy with celiac disease who can't eat gluten, I'm in the "smell but don't eat" mode. The bakery team of leaders and trainees creates a place where the two worlds of "running a business" and "gang culture" clash the most. I was soon thrust into having to make clear and nonnegotiable work rules that are commonplace elsewhere but go straight against the instinct of gang-member thinking: to work only with my homie ("guy from my gang"), not the opposing gang. We have to weigh carefully how many trainees from a certain gang are in the bakery so that no one group dominates, no one group feels that they will "get their way."

I also learned that when trainees are in the initial "healing" phase of our eighteen-month program, they are most open to being in relationship with others and, because of this, they feel a sense of success in themselves. However, once they enter the next phase of the program, entering a business as a trainee, they encounter a different type of stress. Once working in a business, the expectations of a trainee are more akin to the outside world—where they need to be accountable to coworkers and the business results. All this while meeting goals of their service plan of counseling, education, and sobriety. Often it's the work performance that needs to suffer while they work on other aspects of their program. This choice leaves them stressed out. The stress of expectations and of measuring up (in terms of business performance) can sometimes make our homies feel close to leaving Homeboy. When hit by such heavy stress, they might fall back on old habits of gang life. This workplace-stress dynamic led me to see that even though we place a trainee in a business, their challenges are still great and thus managers and supervisors need to wear two hats, the "business" hat and the "mentor" hat. We have to make sure that we have the right managers in place; just average managers would not help our Homeboy trainees—or the programs—to thrive.

Giving People the Freedom to Be Themselves

During the first several weeks of coming to Homeboy, I encountered a whole new set of experiences. I found myself in an enclave that was unlike anything else I'd experienced. From the moment you walk through those doors, you get a sense that people are able to be themselves. There are no airs about them, no pretending, a refreshing attitude of "take me how I am." Despite the fact that they have experienced dramatically more trauma than the average person from the "outside world," they are much more real and accepting of who they are. No matter if they are tall or short, fat or skinny, gay or straight, black or white, pretty or not pretty, have ugly tattoos or cool tattoos. The Homeboy culture has brought them to a place of self-acceptance, knowing that God loves each of them. This authenticity is infectious. Once you visit Homeboy, you'll want to experience more of it.

Comfort with oneself brings with it a natural openness to helping others and a desire to be in community with others. This I found most fascinating. These people have a comfort in themselves that I've not seen in the workplace before. Their sense of, "I'm here and you are here, so let's be in a relationship without wondering, 'What's in it?' for each other" is truly refreshing. This frees people for a natural sharing of emotions, from laughter to crying. Laughing without people judging the laughter. Without fear of going overboard with it or the laughter being inappropriate for the workplace. Crying without being judged as too emotional and without being told that it's a sign of weakness. At Homeboy, when laughter happens, others want to join in, and when crying happens, others want to come and console. People don't stand off to the side as so often happens in workplaces in corporate America.

The other observation and experience that struck me and kept drawing me in like a magnet was people's strong connection to God and their faith. I suppose I was like a lot of other folks on the outside who questioned how violent offenders, those who served long prison terms, could have such a strong faith. Didn't they think that God had forsaken them, considering how awful their lives had been? Yet here I was, standing every day in a sanctuary of spirituality, where people of all faiths openly talked about their faith, openly admitted that without their God, they would not be able to stay on this path. They have thought through how God has been with them their whole life and that by staying true to their faith, life would be better. I quickly realized that all of them were way more advanced in their faith than I had assumed.

Homeboy is a place where people discover their faith and nurture it, making it stronger. Yet it's not a religious organization. We don't teach religion, we do not have Bible study, we don't debate religious perspectives. Even though Greg is a Jesuit priest, we receive no funding from the Archdiocese of Los Angeles; in fact, we pay his salary and benefits. Father Greg speaks about Homeboy being soaked in spirituality, and indeed it is, in what he refers to as exquisite mutuality. A mutuality with one another, within each person's faith, regardless of what that faith may be.

Early on, when I knew it was Father Greg's turn to give the thought of the day, I would make sure to volunteer on those days. In his talks, he would present God in new and refreshing ways. A God of infinite love, a God of mercy, a God of joy, a God too busy loving us to spend time judging us. A God we should give our hearts to. Now these are not new concepts, but the way Greg puts these into perspective of everyday life makes these notions accessible, leads one to think, "Yes, I believe!"

Greg provides these messages without all the structures, traditions, and traps that exist within formal religious institutions, such as the way these messages are often muddled in sermons if you are Catholic or in other religious communities. In fact, I've heard people say on a number of occasions that while Greg is a priest, "he isn't really a practicing Catholic priest." I hear this and I want to defend him, but in keeping with his authentic nature, he just lets the comments slide by. (Jesuits actually take an extra vow of fidelity to the pope, and by the way, our current pope is a Jesuit.) This ham-fisted claim comes mostly from non-Catholic Christians. The most respectful interpretation of this is how when Greg talks about God and instructs us on the meaning of the message, it's a message of a universal God, a God accessible to all. So, his message radiates and resonates with people of many religions, and some critics want to claim God as exclusively their own.

The consistency of these messages from Father Greg flows all the way through Homeboy and is the center of our culture. So when a newcomer arrives, the knowledge is imparted easily and not just by Father Greg but by the whole team. Imparted in a subtle way. The only time God gets mentioned in a direct way is at our morning meetings, during the thought of the day or the ending prayer. Otherwise, God and spirituality are brought in only when one is talking about oneself.

In my corporate-world days, I never felt able to talk about my spirituality or God. Those of us who tried were either sidelined or told to keep our viewpoints to ourselves. That is the way of corporate America; it's a very secular culture and wants to stay that way. While we have a notion of religious freedom and we can't be discriminated against for our religion, the unwritten rule is not to talk about God at work. So, being the guy focused on my career, I understood that rule and followed it completely. I never talked about my view of God and my own spirituality. In practice, there are guardrails you can push with friends on sensitive subject matter—such as one's sex life, political views, marital issues, social problems—and be safe, but don't ever get close to talking about God. What's interesting about this is that a fair number of the very senior executives I worked with over the years were church or synagogue "goers," yet there was hardly a mention of it at work. A "separation of church and state" was enforced. So upon arriving at Homeboy, it was a huge and welcome relief for me to be in an organization that allows this freedom of thought and expression. While it would take me years to talk about my own spirituality in public at Homeboy, I was drinking up everyone else's courage and joy in doing so.

How Would I Fit In?

When I first joined Homeboy, I saw everything through the lens of my background: the guy who successfully led three different businesses, the guy whose training was to get in, assess, and make plans going forward. The $6MDM, whose skill was to figure out what needed to be done to better the organization. I was eager to help, ready to get involved, raring to go. But I also had a bit of trepidation. I was a for-profit guy coming into a well-known and well-loved nonprofit. I was a corporate guy, by all means a "rich and well off" guy, a white guy with no understanding of the population that Homeboy served. Furthermore, I was a competitive guy with a zeal to win—going into a place that didn't use the terminology of winning and losing. And I was one more guy coming into an organization that already had a long list of guys with similar backgrounds who had come in previously to help, with varying degrees of success.

Did they think I was yet another guy "pushed onto" the organization by a consultant and the board? From one aspect, I was the right one for this role; in my career I had worked and thrived in similar circumstances. However, my previous professional experiences haunted me. In my first job, I worked for the family-run company and came to understand how the "family" was in charge and that blood is thicker than water. No matter how great a job I did, I would never be family. In my second major job, at Galls, I was to take over for a beloved founder and to navigate the emotional landscape in which people felt that I was pushing out the founder, even though that was his plan. In my third major job, I was to report to the chairman of a three-plus-billion-dollar corporation who had been in the role for more than twenty-five years. Now I am coming to Homeboy to work with a legendary, charismatic, saintly founder; I simply want to come in and help. But from an outside point of view, I knew there might be misperceptions about my intentions.

So I spoke with Father Greg about my anxiety, and he said to me what he says to all new volunteers, and now I say it to all new volunteers as well. His advice was to come in, be part of the community, listen, and learn. From there, knowing how I fit in and knowing how to help the organization would come naturally.

A Different Kind of Business Model

During those first few months as a volunteer, I was able to get a close-up view of what it's like to be a trainee at Homeboy. I also was introduced to the challenges of running businesses with trainees as the main labor force. For instance, in the Homegirl Café, two of the more tenured workers, homegirls Maga and Rosa, went missing over the weekend. Maga and Rosa were good friends and came through the program together. Many of the women in the café looked up to them as role models, for they were inspiring examples of changed lives. It wasn't until later in the week that we heard what happened. The two women had gotten themselves into a really bad situation with some guys. One of the guys was a tagger: he would go around his neighborhood or proactively in a rival's neighborhood and spray gang-related graffiti. Maga and Rosa were in the car with this guy when he decided to stop and tag a church. A man came out of the church to stop the tagging, and a fight broke out. The guy from the car shot and murdered the man. This made both Maga and Rosa accessories to murder. The last part of the story we heard was that Maga was arrested for accessory to murder and Rosa fled and was on the run from the police.

Both women were beloved and had made real progress toward turning their lives around but got themselves into a bad situation. When this news made its way to the café, the whole team was emotionally crushed. For the other homegirls who had befriended these two women, it was a profound loss. They knew that this easily could have been them, for hanging out with the wrong man, not knowing if the man had a gun, not knowing if a fight would ensue—and not ever wanting to be part of such violence again. Our trainees need to be hypervigilant to avoid the many awful situations that might befall them. The managers from the outside who had taken special effort to mentor Maga and Rosa felt agony unlike anything they had experienced before. I hadn't known either woman, but the sense of grief in the café over the next several days was palpable for all of us.

The leaders of the café didn't know what to do next; they were bewildered and distraught. For me, this was an interesting insight, that in such a mission-based environment, when things went wrong with the trainee team, the extent to which the managers internalized the emotions and absorbed the pain of others was intense. The tricky balance of being a leader—drawing personal boundaries and not getting too involved—and being a mentor is quite difficult. I saw that leadership in a people-based, human services, social enterprise is not simply X's and O's or debits and credits. It's also being empathetic, compassionate, and personally centered, all with the resolve to enable people to grow and change.

I learned a lot from attending the daily council meetings facilitated by Father Greg, in which program leaders gathered to talk about what was happening "on the floor." If there were situations with certain trainees who were having problems, the council would discuss what Homeboy could do for them and what other services they might need. I was impressed that an organization would spend so much time (specifically, leadership's time) on helping one specific person. It was during these meetings that I came to see that Homeboy was truly different from a typical business. I would listen to a problem that had occurred with a trainee and think about how I would have handled it in my old life—that is, how much of corporate America would have handled it—and how about 50 percent of the time, it was not at all how Homeboy would choose to handle the situation. The overriding philosophy was to do what was right for that individual without regard for how it might affect the overall organization. This was a real mindblower for me, that we would put an individual's needs ahead of the organization's needs, that we would not be militant with our policies, that we would not be too strict with protocols, and that we would not worry about what we do for one person compared to another.

Another aspect of my business assessment focused on operational processes and the people performing those processes. Again, I spent a considerable amount of time in each of the businesses, observing, listening, and analyzing the various profit-and-loss statements. Some of the strictly business issues were straightforward to address, but I discovered that some of the people-related issues were less so, although they were inextricably linked with the business issues. As I knew my role was to teach and advise the business managers, not just tell them what to do, one of our very first lessons was to pull together a rough set of financial reports to get a picture of where the agency stood (a process that took four to five weeks). This, in and of itself, was a self-diagnostic revealing some of the problems right off the bat.

If you don't have financial reports at the business level, there is no way to know if the business managers are performing. What these first reports showed was that the businesses were losing massive amounts of money to the tune of more than three million dollars in the previous year. Now, it's a bit complicated as to how the business performance is folded into the overall agency, for the businesses are training programs and thereby carry three times more labor costs than normal for-profit businesses. However, a three-million-dollar loss is a huge number when the top-line revenue of the businesses was just five million dollars and the overall agency top-line revenue, eleven million. I was alarmed at that three-million-dollar loss for a number of reasons. First, it happened without anyone really knowing about it, and more important, there was no way the organization could sustain that type of loss over the long term.

My challenge as a volunteer just four weeks into the effort was to get everyone to understand, urgently, that we have a "burning platform" and something needed to be done about it. Some folks were blasé, some folks said that made sense, and others gave me a blank stare. I think the organization got so used to Father Greg figuring out some way to bring in the money in the nick of time that people took it for granted and just stopped worrying about it. At the same time, the businesses were massively underperforming. The front of the house was taking on more and more trainees. In fact, in that year of 2012, Homeboy had a high-water mark of more than 350 trainees in our paid program. That was a full hundred more than the previous year, and in the words of Hector at the board meeting I attended in my first month, "It's F#*$ing chaos, Dog." Yet even our board was unaware of the financial implications.

During this time, the board was just ending the development of a new five-year strategic plan, which had a lot of good long-term strategies. What it didn't have was a set of short-term tactics that would turn the financial picture around in order to realize this new strategy and financial projections. Specifically, it didn't have the right governance in place for proper oversight. All of which, I've come to learn, is quite common with human services, grassroots-based, nonprofit agencies. The development of this strategic plan was facilitated by Gayle Northrop and had both board and management input. That autumn, when I started as a volunteer, Gayle was nearing the end of the assignment and was around the organization quite a bit. We would often meet for a chat over a cup of coffee. I would pick her brain for her knowledge of the players, and she would ask about my business experiences. Gayle had the sense back then that although the strategic plan was a good one, it was missing the "how to implement it" piece within the current organizational environment. (I suspect she was also whispering in Viktor and Father Greg's ear about the need for a CEO.)

I realized that the current organizational environment was very territorial, and although all managers had a zeal to do the mission, each viewed the mission and their role through his or her own lens. The business managers saw themselves as mission managers more than business managers. They took their eyes off the normal metrics of running the business: profit and loss, inventory control, spoilage, shrinkage, overtime pay, customer service, product quality, etc. What I said to them (and thought at the time) was that they needed to be business managers first and mission managers second. That their "part" of the mission was to create an environment where the trainees learn what it's like to work in a business that better represents the outside world, rather than the utterly unique environment where you don't have to make a profit.

A key aspect to this approach was to break down the wall that existed between the businesses and the front of the house. By "front of the house" I mean the program areas where much of the healing, learning, self-discovery, and a sense of belonging takes place. The irony here is that the front of the house had all the experts and resources to help the trainees. They had the navigators (Homeboy supervisors), the case managers, the mental health experts, the educators—all ready and able to help the trainees. The territorial aspect of Homeboy needed to end. In fact, I made a strong statement to the teams that no one person "owns" a trainee or takes credit for a trainee, that it's all of Homeboy that makes the difference. We don't have individual heroes around here.

Many of the people who held positions of authority were from outside the organization. Very few were once clients. Those who were clients and were able to take that step up were rightly held in high regard. In fact, they were the ones who were on the council. What I noticed right away was a natural split that occurred between managers from the outside and those from the inside. Those managers who grew from within saw everything through the eyes of a trainee. These managers looked out for the trainees and made sure they were taken care of, often to the detriment of the health of the overall organization. The outside managers knew their main contribution was that of a traditional skill set of governance, accountability, and process. Outside managers would defer to inside managers on issues revolving around trainees. While this may seem to make sense, the result was often a lack of teamwork, because each had opinions about the others' area that were never heard, so frustrations grew.

In my experience, the hallmark of a great organization is that it achieves a balance of three key value drivers. Like three legs of a stool, if any one of these is out of balance, the organization will struggle to remain upright. First, you need to be successful in the marketplace, driving shareholder value with good financials. That's the financial side. Second, you should provide products and services that customers want and your team is proud of providing. Third, it needs to be a place where people want to work and where their dreams and ambitions come true while they do their jobs.

Homeboy Bakery had a history of fits and starts. In the early years, they had hired an expert baker to make high-quality breads but had found that the person did not have good management skills and didn't understand how to manage trainees in general and former gang members in particular. So they hired a former client with little bakery experience to run the bakery. Shortly thereafter, they discovered that the quality of the baked goods was inconsistent, and the business started losing customers. If your bread is of poor quality, you won't have customers to serve and thus you will not be hiring homies.

It became apparent that there needed to be leadership in place that could do both. So, another change was made. This time the concept was to have a co-management team in place. Hire an outside expert and team him up with a manager from within who was a former trainee. The co-management setup was in place for about a year prior to my joining Homeboy. The outside manager, Walter, was full of excellent bakery experience. In fact, he came from multiple generations of bakers and had really terrific old-world recipes. The inside manager, Carlos, came up through the program, transformed his life, and had great mentorship skills for the newer trainees. Even though both these managers were passionate about their jobs and highly skilled, the structure was doomed from the beginning.

Although "baking bread to hire more homies" has a nice ring to it, it also gives us clues as to the necessary management structure that Homeboy requires to create a balanced stool of three equally strong legs. Walter, the outside expert with all the baking experience, was put in charge. Carlos, who had the respect of the workers and had all the experience with the people, was made his number two. For context, Walter was white and Carlos, Latino. To make matters worse, they paid the white guy well and the Latino guy half as much. This type of pay gap, usually justified by valuing a college degree over lived experience, or past titles over demonstrated employee respect of a manager, is a form of bias that society has been trained to accept as the norm.

It's easy to see now that the management structure that was put in place was one "to hire homies to bake more bread," driven by a profit-first motive, just like many other businesses. If the purpose of the business is that of healing and the priority is to provide jobs and a training program to "to bake bread to hire more homies," then the leadership and power structure of the businesses should reflect that. Without proactively being aware of this and focusing on the purpose of the organization, this dynamic will not change and will be recreated time and again. It can be difficult to see the truth of this issue, especially when you know the people involved and when others around you point to specific aspects of their background to justify the power and pay differential. However, if the goal is to drive away economic racial inequality, we must confront these truths when we see them.

Everyone gives it a good try at Homeboy, since the team is really terrific at making sure doing "the mission" takes top priority, which includes holding personal frustrations in reserve. Carlos and Walter worked hard at becoming a good management team. Carlos learned aspects of how to run a bakery from Walter, and Walter learned a great deal about trainee leadership. All this played out well when everything was running smoothly, but it broke down when problems in the bakery occurred. These problems usually came in two forms: personal issues among the gang members and product-quality issues that led to customer complaints. The management dynamic was constructed so that Carlos should handle the former and Walter the latter.

Breakdowns erupted when the two crossed over, when Walter thought he knew how to better manage people and when Carlos thought he knew how to better manage product quality. These things could be true, but their teams didn't respect instructions that were given outside of the managers' respective areas of expertise. I've noticed that when homies know what they are being told is wrong, they become stubborn and nonresponsive, which exacerbates the frustration of the manager trying to make change happen. When Carlos had the team skip steps in the baking process to get the product out faster, Walter would become upset and feel that no one cared about our reputation as bakers. Likewise, when Walter sometimes managed through yelling and fear, Carlos would get angry and frustrated because he knew how this was re-triggering the trainees. Then, each man had to undo the mistakes of the other. The legs of the bakery stool were much too unstable. The working environment wasn't great; our product quality wavered at times; and both of these weak legs affected our ability to hire more homies into the business.

When each incident occurred, cooler heads would prevail, but eventually there was too much infighting between the teams in the bakery, and a change needed to occur. The solution I knew needed to be implemented was one that would take a long time to achieve. The bakery management team needed to be grown from within and possess a balanced and equal ability to bake bread *and* manage homies.

To create a healthy environment for organizational growth, we needed to grow and cultivate managers who were strong in both skill sets. I had also observed that a fair number of people, while good leaders, were not good managers, or they were working in areas that didn't suit their skill set that well. I think this came about by too often following the thinking that if someone says they would like a certain job, let's give it to them and see how they do. Allow people to have ambitions, give them a chance, because if we don't, no one else will. While this is the sound philosophy for how we work with our trainees, it unfortunately bled into promotion decisions for senior business managers as well.

What is needed for this philosophy to work are two things: first, a strong management-training program to teach people the job and second, a willingness to move someone out of a job after they demonstrate that they can't be successful in it. What I've found in the human-services nonprofit world is that the resources for a management-training program rarely exist and the resolve to move people out of positions just isn't there. Homeboy was in this situation. To be clear, I'm not saying we shouldn't play to people's strengths or allow their dreams to flourish. But for any organization that lives payroll-to-payroll without a deep reservoir of resources, too much of this philosophy will lead the organization to problems that include lack of accountability, resentment, frustration, and financial troubles. For these reasons, I have always been a strong advocate of a merit-based system of advancement in the case of the professional staff.

A new challenge for me was how to reconcile best business practices with the Homeboy reality that not all people come into their jobs with similar life experiences and skill sets; that "opportunities" should not necessarily be given to those who first demonstrate their competency. Life experiences make a difference and should be taken as a higher credential. Over time, we were able to blend these two aspects together successfully. Now we have a terrific team that has grown the business smoothly and continues to provide training opportunities for many people.

Moment of Truth

In December of 2012, when Father Greg asked me to come on board as CEO, we talked about the reporting relationship. Everyone in the organization would report to me, and down the line, Father Greg and I would report to the board. While this is the right way of running the organization from a strategy and day-to-day-operations standpoint, I knew that because Father Greg was the founder and the executive director up until that point, the organization would also be watching how the relationship between Father Greg and me played out. As I dove deeply into the work over the first several months, there was a lot for me to accomplish. A big part of it was understanding the team and understanding what they worked on. It was equally important for them to know who I was, what my philosophy was on how things should run day to day, what information should be communicated to me and/or to Father Greg, and when people could make their own decisions—typical CEO work. As I was going about this, there was always the question in my mind of acceptance. Did the organization really accept a CEO coming in to take on the role that Father Greg had played for the past twenty-five years?

As much as Father Greg did not want to run the day-to-day operations, I don't think people believed that he was the one who wanted to give that up. I think people thought the board wanted Father Greg to hand over his reins to a CEO. Being very conscious of this, I went out of my way to make sure that there wasn't any gap between my decisions and Father Greg's desires for the organization, and to do a few things symbolically to make sure everyone knew we were aligned. At senior staff meetings, Father Greg would always be the one to end the meeting, articulating the overarching vision and goal. Then my job was to facilitate and execute our decisions and plans to ensure that the organization realized successful outcomes in alignment with Father Greg's vision and goals.

When I first came in, without a doubt there was a lot of respect given to me, and that never wavered. Of all the organizations I've approached, Homeboy is starkly different from most other for-profit businesses, where you have to, at least a little bit, earn your way in to gain respect. There are lots of business books written about that. But Homeboy has a different philosophy. The folks here are grateful for people who come to help, and they offered respect and trust right away. The interesting dichotomy is that while I was much respected and deferred to, there was always a secondary vibe that they were worried about what would happen with Father Greg, and they wondered why was I here. Most of it was based on their fear that Father Greg would someday leave the organization. I clearly took on the posture that was so true for me: I'm here just to help Father Greg, and he's going to be here a long time. I'm confident he's going to die in that chair, if I have anything to do with it. His last breath will be taken while helping homies in this organization.

As the weeks and months went by, we got into a nice rhythm, but I always felt that even though the organization believed in me, people there wondered why I was there. Was I there to make myself look better at the expense of the organization, or was I really there to help? People on the senior staff told me stories of outside professionals who, over the years, had come in and tried to make a name for themselves more than help the organization. So the organization was worried that Father Greg would be taken advantage of by some hot-shot corporate guy. That's who I was—the corporate guy. I was a white guy in an organization predominantly with people of color. I had worked at a big corporation, and they were a little nonprofit. I was well-off. I did well monetarily in life, and most of the people there were poor and working for wages below market-based comparable positions. Given these differences, I felt some lingering doubt.

Because I felt that the organization doubted my reasons for being there or kept thinking there was something else behind that, I needed to make sure I was accepted well by my senior team. Homeboy is blessed with so many volunteers and people coming in to offer their services. Michelle was one such person. She is a well-known executive coach who helps CEOs and leaders work on assessments of their people, work on their style, and work on essentially their "flat" spots (i.e., areas of needed improvement and blind spots).

Throughout my career it was normal to have a formal assimilation process for new employees, particularly when a new leader came on. After five months of working at Homeboy, and knowing that Michelle was offering her services pro bono, I decided to ask her to help conduct an assimilation process for me. The plan was to choose ten of my direct reports, along with Father Greg, and interview them about me. She would discover what questions they had about me, which I presumed would include questions about my reasons for being there. At the end of that interview process, we would sit together as a team, and she would bring these issues up in a confidential way so we could talk through them. She spent a few weeks on it and along the way, gave me anonymous insights about people's feelings. Then it culminated in one of our traditions at Homeboy, which is to get into kinship around the dinner table.

We sat around a square table in the café, and Michelle led the discussion. As we proceeded, I was surprised to learn that almost none of the feedback had to do with whether or not they accepted me, because she discovered that they clearly did. It also had nothing to do with whether they respected me; they clearly did. It had more to do with why I was even asking them these questions. People at Homeboy care about people so much that they're not going to judge me for who I've been or what they thought my intentions were. They respected what I was doing for them. What they wondered the most was why I would be questioning them about *their* respect for me?

As for my concern about being a white male in an organization where nearly everyone else is a person of color, the team just said, "Don't worry about it. That's not a problem." Obviously, Father Greg stepped forward and said, "That's not a problem," too. What was heartwarming about that process was that I was able to accept and believe that we are one team, that we all have a shared vision and a shared mission. They see me as the leader of the team and, in the end, the worry about acceptance had more to do with my own thoughts and concerns than the way the team treated me or reacted to me. There was so much work to be done to help our trainees transform their lives and to put the organization on a solid footing; I realized that my own concerns were so very inconsequential.

The Careful Move Forward

I could see that there was a lot of hard work ahead of me; there would be no quick fixes. I needed to commit to being there for an extended period of time. So much basic organizational realignment, process improvement, and financial rigor needed to be implemented. I needed to figure out how to get the organization behind these efforts without imparting the impression I was changing the organization from what Father Greg wanted. I was in a people-oriented, take-care-of-everybody culture, and I needed to make hard decisions as to who should stay and who should go. It was clear to me that the organization was not going to make it if we didn't change. I was going to work as hard as I ever had to make sure Homeboy didn't fail.

As much as people welcomed me and asked for help, I felt a lot of protective eyes on us, watching how I treated Greg and how he treated me. My relationship with Greg grew stronger during this first year. I went out of my way not to take over for him and never sat in his chair during council when he was away—to this day I have never sat in his chair. I would send him weekly updates and ask him to spend more time in the office, but he stayed away to give me space to work.

It was during this time that I started to have weekly executive-team meetings, and I found myself developing real relationships with people I never would have imagined. Through these relationships and the executive team, we made the changes necessary to get through the year and then started working on how to get to long-term stability. We downsized the staff by twelve people and lowered the head count of trainees from 250 to 190 over a six-month time frame. All hard choices but we needed to survive through the end of the year so we could be there for the next year.

Father Greg's advice to listen, learn, and become part of the community was good advice for me because it made me pause and slow down. It made me recognize when to listen, when to learn, and—after a good amount of time—when to make changes so that we could evolve into a stronger organization.

While I began to make organizational changes for the long term, being part of the Homeboy community filled me with exuberance. At the same time, the full frame of the dark underside of the larger society—the America I thought I knew—was coming into view, which awakened an energy in me I had never known before. But it broke my heart, because the magnitude of the destruction, darkness, speciousness, and hopelessness it created was beyond anything I had seen before.

CHAPTER 5

A TALE OF TWO AMERICAS

One afternoon while I was spending time in the Homeboy gift shop, a homie I was working with shared a concern about a homegirl in our program. She was not eating and was becoming unhealthy. I learned that the money she was earning from her full-time job wasn't enough to cover her rent, food, and diapers for her children. She chose not to eat so that her baby would have diapers. I looked into the eyes of this woman's friend and saw the love and despair. A sense of urgency rose in me: we had to find a solution. People should not be forced to choose between basic necessities. Later that day, I spoke with Father Greg and shared with him the situation and my concern. He looked at me and said, "Ah, the tyranny of diapers." I was knocked backward. I now had these two "tyranny" phrases locked in my head. Who was this tyrant that demanded pennies for shareholders while simultaneously forcing people to choose which basic need to meet and which to neglect?

I was stunned to see the type of healthcare the poor have in what is nothing less than the Forgotten America. A manager of ours chose not to have his wife on our healthcare plan because of the costs to him—our plan was better and at a lower cost than the corporate plan I had been on at Aramark. So when his wife was having difficulty with a growing cyst, he took two days off and took his wife to Tijuana so she could have it removed—for cash. One thing led to another, and she had to go to Tijuana two more times before finally telling us what was going on. We found a local doctor here who would help her (for cash, and not the concierge kind). I came to realize that this case wasn't the exception. In fact, we had many others who didn't subscribe to our healthcare plan. The most often cited reason? To save money. As was the case with a staff member who declined to subscribe so she could save money for her children. We raised her pay to cover the difference, but she still didn't take the coverage. We finally convinced her to pick up the coverage some months later—just before she was diagnosed with cancer.

While the rest of us might judge these two people for not having coverage, we really don't understand the pressure they are under to just get by. They often must choose between basic needs while coping with a 50 percent higher likelihood of having a common mental health disorder, such as depression or anxiety.[8] It is common that they view their lives as less important than the lives of their children and other people in the family who depend on them.

Dentistry—oh my, this is another area of great need and little or no access. There are a lot of scoundrels who take advantage of our people. I can't tell you how many times a homie would come in with severe mouth pain and tell us they went to a dentist, paid cash, then the dentist pulled the tooth and now the wound is infected. Upon hearing the full story, it's a bit suspect that they needed the tooth pulled in the first place, and infections happen more often than they should. Even those who sign up for healthcare coverage get lost in the maze of paperwork and bureaucratic morass, and in no way do they have the fortitude to be strong healthcare advocates for themselves. Even those of us who have been privileged with better circumstances become intimidated by all the forms, multiple vendors, and difficult-to-read statements involved in our healthcare. How can we expect more from those who are already beaten down by systems and circumstances?

One of our homegirls, Pauline, an African American in her forties, recently died of a heart attack after having heart surgery a year ago. I have no doubt that if she had been my daughter with the same medical history, she would be alive today. We in the Privileged America know how to get the right care, treatment, and recuperation. Pauline's story for me is more about what is wrong with our society. She led a tragic life, and every time she tried to do better

8. World Health Organization, "Breaking the Vicious Cycle between Mental Ill-Health and Poverty" (September 4 2007), https://www.who.int/mental_health/policy/development/ 1_Breakingviciouscycle_Infosheet.pdf.

to overcome the obstacles, barriers, and challenges, she just couldn't get there. The problem was part mental illness, part being stuck in the downward spiral of gang life. Nevertheless, she was a kind person who was joyous but filled with pain. Addiction is a terrible thing. She lost her job with us and other companies because of it. When she was clean, she worked on getting better, and yet the challenges kept growing. Addiction thrives when the amount of debt increases; it loves the constant threat of electricity being turned off. Holding off addiction when there are children to be taken care of and one is short on money is sometimes too much for a person to do all alone.

On one occasion she was short on money to take care of her family. At Homeboy we give a lot of money away to help in such circumstances, sometimes providing short-term loans to our people if we have the money to give. At this time, she needed a few hundred dollars to make a car and utility payment, but we didn't have money in the bank to lend her. Our case managers did the "right thing" by saying, "We can't help now but we can next week" (when more donations were expected). On the following Monday, Pauline was in tears, talking to her case manager. She'd become so desperate over the weekend that she prostituted herself to get the money she needed. Think about the depth of desperation a person must feel to make such a choice—and then come in the following week with a huge sense of shame. Try to resist the urge to justify her predicament: "She shouldn't have had the car loan," or "She shouldn't have spent her money without holding some back for utilities." It comes down to simply this: our society is set up in such a way that the "poor" must turn tricks to get by. How can we let this happen? A human being prostituted herself just because she was trying to make ends meet. She tried doing it the "right way," but the challenges were too great, the hurdles too high. How can this be acceptable in the United States of America?

I often think about what I could have done differently to help Pauline. I carry these thoughts every day. It took me a while to learn not to judge people in these types of situations but to just help the person who is in front of me today who has tragically tough choices to make. Pauline's life was a real tragedy, but when I talked to Pauline, it was pureness—pure joy or pure sadness—no airs, no false pretenses, no bitterness. She made me feel good and reinforced my belief that there is God's goodness in all of us. My life is enriched by having known Pauline. My heart is broken that we could not have done more for her.

In California, four in ten Americans live below the poverty line when you factor in the cost of living, including housing and income that includes housing subsidies, food stamps, and wages.[9] [10]

The additional barrier our former gang members and ex-prison inmates face is how hard it is to qualify for clean and safe housing, despite having paid their debt to society. The concept of a livable wage is critical when more than 69 percent of one's income, when making minimum wage in California, goes to pay rent. Fifty percent of Black and Brown communities disproportionately make up the population of poor Californians. The trade-offs and choices our folks must make each month when the bills are due are often insurmountable.

In a rudimentary way of saying it, at Homeboy we pay people to work on themselves. For we know that a person who has just left the prison system and who doesn't want to go back to their gang needs a job to provide food and shelter. It's nearly impossible for them to get a job upon release, and if they do, holding on to it is nearly as hard. They've been victims of so much trauma that they are not resilient enough to hold down a job. We need to help them truly heal. To do so, they need enough money for food and shelter, or else they will return to their gang to make money, and we will lose them again to the poverty and trauma cycle.

"Baking more bread to hire more homies" means we put more people to work while teaching them skills, including how to work with one another. Selling our goods at the farmers market is one of those jobs that builds confidence. It really teaches our folks how to interact with the public, to not be shy, to look people in the eyes, to smile, to be considerate, and to sell bread. Mostly, it's a place that helps reframe the meaning of work from something that is demeaning into something that is empowering.

---

9. Elijah Chiland, "Accounting for Housing Costs, California Has the Nation's Highest Poverty Rate," *Curbed Los Angeles* (September 14, 2018), https://la.curbed.com/2018/9/14/17856870/california-poverty-rate-housing-cost-of-living.

10. Sarah Bohn, Caroline Danielson, and Tess Thorman, "Poverty in California," Public Policy Institute of California (July 2020), https://www.ppic.org/publication/poverty-in-california/.

The amazing thing about our farmers market is that it's an all-cash business. I often smile when I talk about our farmers market business model because most people in the for-profit business of corporate America would cringe at how we go about it. Essentially, what happens each day is guys in charge of a particular market pick up their bread and pastries from our bakery, drive out to the market, set up their tent, sell the bread, sell the pastries, take the money in—which is all-cash—come back, deposit the cash, bring back the leftover bread, and fill out a report. It's that simple. Any corporate auditor would look at the lack of processes we have in place with this operation and have a conniption. There are many non-controllable events and processes that have the potential to be out of control with this operation. In the end, it's Homeboy Industries. The people who work in our markets are so thankful to have a job and to be part of our program, where they're changing their lives, that they don't steal from their own house. They are perhaps the most trustworthy of all the workers I've dealt with in my career; they do the right thing.

One of the other things I've learned firsthand at Homeboy is how hard it is to find and keep work if you're a felon, if you're on parole, or if you have debt. How hard it is to actually do an honest day's job. For instance, there was Gregory, a middle-aged guy who had been in and out of prison his whole life. He came to Homeboy a couple of times before it stuck. Eventually, Gregory became our lead seller at farmers markets in and around Los Angeles. He was one of our best sellers in fact. He had a good gift of gab, created a base of regular customers at the markets, and would sell out of product nearly all the time. His markets were on Thursday, Friday, Saturday, and Sunday. I remember him coming in to talk to the bakery manager one day while I was standing within earshot. I heard him say, "I can't do my markets this weekend. We need coverage from somebody else." The manager said, "Why can't you make it this weekend?" I'm thinking he must be planning a vacation or something else that other people do when they're asking for time-off in advance. No.

What he did that weekend was turn himself in. He had incurred debts while incarcerated and on parole. He had to pay for his correction officer and outstanding court fees. One way to pay off those debts is to "earn time." He chose to spend four days in jail because he didn't have enough money to pay those debts. You see, he was trying to save all his money because he had custody of his two children and wanted to ensure he could afford basic necessities, such as rent, so he could keep them. He was on his own with his two children, and he chose to go to jail for those four days. When I first heard that, I was like, "Wow! I didn't realize that situation occurred." That seemed like a pretty mature response, and he was setting his priorities right.

The following week came along, after he had gone to county jail for those four days. I was talking to him and asked, "Did everything work out okay?" He hesitated, then told me that part of the tough decision was that his children were ages thirteen and eight, and his arrangements had fallen through, so he had to leave them alone in their apartment for those four days. Understandably, he was worried and stressed the whole time. Now, he's thinking maybe he should have tried to find the money or borrow the money, as opposed to leaving his children alone. I mention this part of the story because it's not so clear what the right decision is for these men and women who have these challenges. They want to do right, but the system is sometimes stacked against them when navigating how to do right all the time. Was he right for going to jail to pay off his debt? Sure. Was he right to do it while he left his children alone? That's not a clear yes or no. I'm not sure what I would've done in that situation, and it's hard for me to get my brain wrapped around it. This moment was another that cemented the fact that our trainees have a whole host of problems different from any I've ever had.

The Forgotten America: The Mentally Ill

Confounding the barriers is the effect of mental illness among the poor. In 2019, Los Angeles' point-in-time count found that 79 percent of the unsheltered reported or were observed to have a mental illness (including PTSD), a substance-abuse issue, or a physical disability. Many of our homies were previously incarcerated and unsheltered and come out of incarceration and off the streets in need of mental-health care. Researchers agree that it isn't mental illness that causes people to become unsheltered or homeless; rather, it's poverty and a lack of affordable housing that are the primary drivers. A UCLA study also found that 92 percent of those who have been homeless for more than three years also have a health condition, ranging from those that are preventable and treatable to those that are more serious and complex, such as cancer. What we have is a system of structural barriers that creates and perpetuates lack of access to the most fundamental needs of those in poverty. Nearly every study and measurement highlights the disproportionate effects these barriers have on Black and Brown communities, women, and children.

Carmen, a stereotypical "Chola" in her dress and manner, now in her fifties, is a homegirl from the early days. She ran with gangs, was addicted for many years to drugs, lived on the streets, and had a few stints at Homeboy. She has anger problems and some type of mental illness. At only four feet eight inches tall, she is a bundle of energy. When she is stable, she is so very sweet. She knows many homies from when they were little and is adored by many. Carmen has struggled with homelessness her whole adult life. A few times she was able to get government housing but lost it because of her behavior when she stopped taking her meds. It is so clear what needs to happen. She needs adult supervision to make sure she is safe, housed, and taking her medications as prescribed. Yet that doesn't happen in our society. She is left to fend for herself on the streets. We've talked to county officials many times, and they say their hands are tied. She is estranged from her family. They can't handle her. Her son was able to get out of the neighborhood to make a better life for himself, and he can't have her around his young children. The best part of my day is when Carmen shows up at our offices and walks around to give everyone a hug, to give *me* a hug. The joy in her hugs is real. I love talking to her about the old Mexican homeopathic concoctions for any illness you can think of. Whatever money she has, she always makes a meal and shares it with someone. In many ways, Carmen is my inspiration to keep moving forward with the work. How can we make a better life for Carmen? When we see her on the outs, it is just heartbreaking.

The story of Carmen is not just a one-off. She is among the unfortunate who slip through society's cracks. There are hundreds and thousands of people we see every year with similar conditions. It was eye-opening for me to see that our society lets so many people who have serious mental illness walk the streets on their own with no support. I had always assumed that some government entity would take care of these people and not abandon them into the forgotten abyss. Men and women are being released from prison when the authorities know they have no family support whatsoever and are just left to be on their own. No one ensures that they have a place to stay or makes sure they take their medicines. As I type this, I can imagine the calls from those in charge, telling me, "Of *course*, there is a program," citing the government regulations providing for such services. My point is that while this support might technically exist on paper, it doesn't in practice. Somehow, these mysterious programs are always overloaded with cases for the people Homeboy serves. Those with tattoos, those who are gang affiliated, and those who have committed violent offenses are the ones who never get access to these limited resources. They are left to fend for themselves or rely upon their gang to help them, hence the vicious cycle continues.

Most times, for the mentally ill there is no place for them to stay unless they voluntarily take their medicine. While I understand this rule, it has many negative consequences and contributes to chronic homelessness and further mental illness. Our society must do better. Even the great team at Homeboy is not able to help severely mentally ill people because we do not have medically trained professionals. So we just help the individuals as much as we can and try to find others to help—it's mostly a lost cause.

All across America, there is a homelessness crisis, and Los Angeles has among the worst situations. Every night in Los Angeles County, fifty-eight thousand people are homeless. Fifty-eight thousand is a huge number—breathtaking and heartbreaking in size and scale. Much has been written about this and a lot of money has been poured into various solutions, yet the problem still exists. Too many of us have become numb to this fact of life for the Forgotten America: homelessness lurks just around the corner. It is caused by a job loss, an expensive medical event, separation from a spouse, an extra mouth to feed, a domestic violence situation, a redevelopment of the neighborhood, and the list goes on. There are not enough shelters to help people. I had felt that in my time at Homeboy I had seen nearly everything and witnessed a lot of awful situations. That was until a few years ago when I spent a couple of afternoons on Skid Row as part of my duties as a board member of the local Salvation Army. Mind you, this is only a mile from where I go every day for work at Homeboy. During those two afternoons, I was sickened to see the conditions that homeless people are forced into. While they might have enough food, they don't have clean living conditions. That we, as the most prosperous nation in the history of the world, do not take care of our people—it's sinful.

Over 70 percent of the Homeboy population are definitionally homeless, meaning they do not have stable and secure housing. As many are intentionally leaving the gang lifestyle, they need to live away from their families who put them into this situation. So they go live with friends or relatives, essentially couch surfing. A fair number of our people rent a bed in a sober living house. These houses have popped up all over Los Angeles. In the house, you share a bedroom with three to four other adults and must abide by sober living rules the house establishes. Overall, this is a good business and housing model, and it works out fine for those on the Westside of Los Angeles. However, as with most so-called services to which our population fights for access, they end up with unethical providers and find themselves bouncing around in search of stability. They spend six hundred dollars a month for a bed and are in a house that is overcrowded and dirty, and the sobriety aspect is often forgotten or unenforced. Definitely a situation that doesn't help a person's transformation to a better life.

The current construct of "taking care of the poor" is an interesting one. It implies we should (or are expected to) take care of everyone who is poor. However, there is so much research and so many examples of how we take excellent care of those most like us, those of us in the Privileged America. A research article on public support of poverty policies highlights the commonly held assumption that those in poverty are there due to individualist contributions, meaning, they put themselves there.[11] . . . And thus we tend not to help those people. However, structural contributions to poverty (such as a lack of living wages, little or no access to healthcare, unaffordable housing)

---

11. Jodi Masters, PhD student, Pepperdine University, Critique of a Scholarly Work: *Predicting Support for Welfare Policies: The Impact of Attributions and Beliefs about Inequality* (2020), https://drive.google.com/file/d/1j49XEbWohvicHGE2IvwDDm18AFcH3v24/view?usp=sharing.

and contemporary attributions (which may include intergenerational poverty implications and social worlds, such as gang life) are the root causes. It should be noted that inequality, specifically income disparity, contributes just as much to the issue as anything else.

Topics such as universal healthcare, affordable housing, medical treatment for nonphysical issues (i.e., mental illness), a livable wage, crime, hardship on businesses are all we hear about from our political leadership at the moment. Our country is so divided and polarized. Are we willing to seek the truths of these individualistic-versus-structural narratives? Perhaps what we've forgotten (or choose not to look at due to cognitive dissonance) is our collective values as a nation (i.e., the values we share as Americans). What of the Golden Rule, which has a version in nearly every religion? What unifies us; what might allow us to even begin to have this discussion in the first place? Might it be that most of us have lent money or helped someone out at least once in our lives and that if we didn't, they may not have been able to get on their feet again? Might it be that the challenges of loved ones have led to death, financial loss, addiction, and other insurmountable consequences? Might it be that we ourselves have been in this spot at one time or another and were fortunate enough to have the support of someone in a position to do so? How do we get to a place where we can hear each other? See each other? Cocreate new types of government–private sector–civil society contracts? How might we pool our collective intelligence to solve these structural problems? The Forgotten America is the dark side of us.

I'm haunted by the stories of those such as Pauline's, Carmen's, and Gregory's. They are what drive me forward.

Generational Poverty and Violence

As I dove deep into my work to address the challenges on the business and financial security side of enterprise, I endeavored to continue learning about the mission of Homeboy, life at Homeboy, how that part of the work gets done. I did this by actively attending and participating at council. It is always instructive and insightful for me to listen and pay attention to how our team thinks about each individual trainee and particularly how Father Greg teaches each of us along the way. It truly takes a team of people talking through each trainee's circumstances every day so that no one falls through the cracks. True to human nature, one trainee might tell their health therapist their concerns, another might tell a case manager their concerns, and yet another might tell a navigator their concerns. The expert team at council goes about blending all those stories together to tease out a complete picture and how best to give that trainee what he or she needs.

Many topics the council deals with are the specific setbacks our trainees experience. Setbacks such as being treated unfairly by their parole officer, being regulated by their gang (being beaten up by the gang for attempting to leave them), having the utility bill come due with no money available, being denied child visitation by an estranged partner, being plagued by sexual identity issues, being demeaned by a parent, encountering fights outside Homeboy—the list goes on and on. All of which have an outsized impact when someone is so fragile while trying to move their life forward in a good and sincere way.

Always at council, one of the hardest topics to deal with is domestic violence. Too many times, we've had to discuss the best course of action for our female trainees who keep getting beaten up by the men in their lives. Very often, nearly all the time, the abuser is not in our program. So it's a little bit easier to help the trainee by providing a sanctuary, a place of safety, so that when she comes to work each day she knows, and we know, that she is safe. Our council team is great about finding resources and providing therapy to help these women navigate away from these traumatizing relationships. Domestic violence remains a core issue within our community because it is a core issue in gang life and in prison. What I've come to learn is that for recovering gang members who are trying to change their lives around, a first step toward healing means confronting their early complex trauma during childhood, complex trauma from growing up in a gang environment, and complex trauma from being in prison. There is a generational cycle to this violence, and the abused almost always become abusers, one way or another.

We run a CGA (Criminal and Gang Members Anonymous) class, similar to an AA (Alcoholics Anonymous) or NA (Narcotics Anonymous) program, because we believe that being in a gang is an addiction problem and violence is an addiction problem, just as substance abuse is an addiction problem. For our folks, the sequence of giving things up usually goes something like this: they give up gang life, they give up crime, they give up drugs, and usually the last thing they give up is beating their woman or abusing their children. In some ways, that's their last form of control.

I think we do a phenomenal job of helping people navigate these tough transitions as they move through their recovery pathways. Most of the time it is the women within our population who deal with domestic violence most frequently, although it happens to some of our men too, usually within the baby mama or baby daddy dynamic. There are times when we must draw a line and say they can't be in our program any longer if they don't leave that person or leave a situation where they abuse another. We provide the financial resources that enable them to leave. However, after a certain point, after we have provided therapy and other resources, if they still choose this type of behavior, we need to draw a line.

Some of the most difficult discussions at council relating to domestic violence are those regarding known abusers in our program. In my early days at Homeboy, when it was revealed that some guy was an abuser, my initial response was, "If we know he abuses somebody, let's just fire him." I'd say, "Why are we even talking about keeping this guy on our payroll? Why are we keeping him working in our businesses? Why are we keeping him in our training program?" The answer was and remains fairly simple and straightforward. We know, first of all, that this person is coming to us for help. It's not like he's denying his problem. And we know that if we don't help that person, there's no other organization in the county that's going to help him, and that guy is going to keep on beating that woman. For us, it's important to work with him, to look for progress along the way. That's core to our mission. Even though he's an abuser, we don't demonize him, we don't forget about him—we work to help him. We look for the goodness in him and nurture that goodness so that he can heal and end his cycle of violence.

So when we say that we "work with the hardest of hardest cases," it is because the difference between life and death is greatest among these folks. It is a Homeboy priority to stop this cycle of violence within our community, and we work hard to do that. It's also hard to explain this to people who stop at the top-line, individualistic narrative. For example, I remember a time we were invited to speak to a UCLA graduate business class on the topic of social entrepreneurship. It was in the spring, one semester, not too long ago. As Father Greg and I arrived to give our talk, we entered the lecture hall and stood near the podium. I looked at all the faces in the crowd, rising upward toward the ceiling in stadium-style seating. There were about eighty MBA students, who had most likely worked elsewhere and were taking this course to advance their careers along a more "mission driven" path. I wondered if they had seminal moments of their own and saw social enterprise as a tool toward that purpose.

At the end of our talk, we held a Q&A session. It just happened to be at a time when we were dealing with a difficult and rare challenge of an abuser and his victim working simultaneously within our organization. As a team, we were working through the variety of issues that underpinned this challenge. Things like how to keep them separate and safe, how to provide the best access to a variety of mental health support and resources, and assisting them with technical issues, such as working through the court proceedings of restraining orders. Father Greg and I are sitting near the podium when all of a sudden, he chooses to tell the story of this young man, the abuser, and how we're helping him overcome the last leg of his addiction. Then the phrases *sexual predator* and *violent predator* come up. In that moment, I lift my head and look at the audience. I see that they are aghast that we would help this young man. I know the looks on their faces. They are thinking, *Why would you even consider having an abuser work for you?* Father Greg, being true to who he is (not just defiant but rebellious), addresses the crowd, knocking down the notion that there's evil in this trainee. He says, "He just needs help." He and others like him need a therapeutic program to break this cycle of violence.

The first three or four questions on this topic were from women, who, rightly so, kept asking us how we keep the workplace safe and why we would keep somebody like that on staff. To the former question, safety is a top concern, and if we feel that we cannot keep someone safe, we ask that person to leave the program. To the latter question, there's no right or wrong answer to this. What we know is that, at the deepest, truest level, no person is evil, and every person is good. That everyone deserves a chance to overcome the violence of their past and to heal so that the cycle of violence has a chance of being broken. We take a countercultural, even rebellious, stand against the grain of our society. We know that if we don't help that person, it's likely no one else will and that person will just spin more out of control. We are going to help each and every person; that is our mission, that is what makes Homeboy special. I have learned so much from these truths during my time there.

Proof of Flourishing, Proof That Business Can Make a Difference

When people come into our program, they are essentially broken: abused, untrusting, fearful, and feeling that they don't fit into society. And all for good reason—for they have heard a constant message of being unfit and they have been disappointed by so many adults already. Our first task is to say yes, that we can help them and offer a safe environment so that they can begin to trust again. It's only later in their time with us that the emphasis switches to working on oneself and to believe in their own innate goodness. So much healing needs to take place. They are victims of complex trauma. They have been abused repeatedly: physically, sexually, and emotionally. Their background stories vacillate between periods of being victims of trauma to periods of desired reconciliation to intervals of incarceration. Yet their transformations are like watching modern-day miracles. They have faced their demons; they have worked through their pain; they have overcome all sorts of society's obstacles. They have suffered more, toiled more, gotten "off the mat" more than anyone would have believed or thought possible. They have separated themselves from their families. They have lived in shelters. They have gone hungry; they have very few possessions; they have endured indignities. All this to get to the other side, to the side of life that you and I call normal. The life we take for granted is the one they so desperately want. To live a simple life. A life whereby they feel that they fit in, and when they get there, it's awesome to see. In many ways it sneaks up on them. At first it starts by having only a few good days every now and then, until finally, most days are good days and only every now and then a bad one sneaks in. And when that bad day happens, they realize it and have the resilience not to let it take them sideways. That is when transformation really locks in.

As you form relationships with these brave men and women, you become a part of their community, and you bear witness to their goodness and their resilience. There is a special sweetness, an ebullience that comes with seeing just the small instances of change and normalcy, like when they shyly ask if they can take time off to go to their children's school for a holiday parade, or when they ask for help in setting up a bank account, or when they excitedly tell you they received an A on their take-home quiz for school. All very commonplace, and yet it was never part of their life before Homeboy. The proof of flourishing is in the mundane. The sweetness is in seeing them grow and thrive and push their lives forward. All anchored in their belief in their own goodness. A true miracle.

It wasn't until I started at Homeboy that I quickly realized there really are two Americas. In the Forgotten America live the poor, the despised, and the demonized who struggle for decent housing, education, and—regretfully—medical care beyond emergency services. In the Privileged America, where the rest of us live, we often take for granted access to these basic needs. It breaks my heart to know that with all the successes our American society has produced, we still have a national poverty rate of 12 percent. That means 38.1 million Americans cannot afford basic necessities.[12] As bad as that seems, when one looks at the numbers more closely, they will discover that some subsets of those in poverty have it even worse than others. Women are affected by poverty at a greater rate than men, and children even more so. If you are nonwhite, the likelihood of poverty increases even more. The poverty rate is nearly double that of the national average for Hispanics, African Americans or Blacks, and Native Americans.[13] One in four people living with a disability is living in poverty. Teetering on the edge of poverty, another 93.6 million

---

12. Jessica Semega, Melissa Kollar, John Creamer, and Abinash Mohanty, "Income and Poverty in the United States, 2018," United States Census Bureau, September 10, 2019, https://www.census.gov/library/publications/2019/demo/p60-266.html.

13. United States Conference of Catholic Bishops, "Poverty by Race," *Poverty USA*, https://www.povertyusa.org/data.

people—about 30 percent of our population—hold on tight to a rope that can snap at any time.[14]

Looking at these statistics, it's easy to forget that each and every one of these numbers represents a real person who has hopes and dreams for themselves and for their children, just as you and I do. If you dare to look even deeper, you'll see folks like our people, our homeboys and homegirls, whose circumstances statistically guarantee a very high likelihood of being incarcerated, becoming addicts, becoming sexually exploited, becoming trapped in a structure in which it seems only divine intervention, such as Father Greg and Homeboy Industries, might offer hope. The most disheartening aspect of this structural inequality is that these folks, who have done their time, who are ready and looking for a fresh start, cannot access the very things they need to position themselves out of poverty. Most do not qualify for welfare, public housing, affordable healthcare, employment, and university loans because they have a criminal record. We are the richest country on earth and continue to trap our poor in the poverty-to-prison pipeline.

I have now had an up-close, front-row seat on how we take care of the poor, and it's awful. As a committed capitalist, I believe the business community needs to take a more active role; it can't simply expect the government to solve the problem. People are not poor by choice. For the vast majority, being born into poverty puts them into this situation: lack of institutional support, complex trauma, generational poverty, oppressive public policies designed to perpetuate the structure. The "American Dream" is there for the lower middle class on up. Poor people and those on the margins cannot bootstrap their way forward because there are too many barriers. Imagine how overwhelming your life would be in this situation—and add to that the inability to afford healthcare.

I became part of a team that fights every day against the notion perpetuated by the Privileged America—that some people are less important than others. But the team had very limited resources—other than the will not to give up. I've discovered that I cannot give up either. Now, having seen up close in an

---

14. United States Conference of Catholic Bishops, "Poverty among Adults with Disabilities," *Poverty USA*, https://www.povertyusa.org/facts.

unvarnished way how society treats fellow human beings, I am resolved to do something to help. Through Greg's teachings I know that "something" doesn't have to be grand or seismic, just whatever might help the person sitting in front of me needing comfort or advice in each present moment.

What gives me strength is witnessing the resiliency of our people. Even when they come to the harsh realization that everything is stacked against them, they do not give up. In my first few months here, I started to see and understand the notion and specialness of being in kinship with the poor. Of being in relationship with people who truly have great faith. I started to understand that I was no better than them—in fact in many ways, I was worse off, for I had pretenses and didn't know my true self.

My faith was awakening.

CHAPTER 6

HOW GENEROSITY AND GRATITUDE MAKE
A WAY FOR GRACE

Dorothy Day, social activist and cofounder of the Catholic Worker movement, said in her autobiographical book, *The Long Loneliness*, "I longed for a church near at hand where I could go and lift up my soul."[15] For me, Homeboy lifted up my soul without my even realizing it. The day I walked through those doors, I began a journey I never planned on taking. Being around Father Greg is a privilege, and my early goal was to soak up as much as I could from him. What I found in Greg is a truly authentic person of God with an unwavering commitment to his view: God is too busy loving us to be judging us. There is no such thing as an evil person. And no one should ever be defined by the worst thing they have ever done.

As I witnessed Father Greg's actions and words, I was in awe at how he'd use conventional wisdom in a different context that seemed incredibly insightful. For example, "We treat gang members, not gangs." Or "The gang is an addiction like alcohol. You don't go to a bar and recruit patients; you wait for them to be ready." So, in Father Greg's words: "You need to treat the patient, not for the cough but for the underlying issue. The underlying issues behind joining a gang are despair, trauma, and sometimes mental illness."

While my analytical brain was processing these new ideas and concepts about the plight of the poor and the existence of the Two Americas, my spiritual brain was being remade by the lessons of being in the Homeboy

---

15. Dorothy Day, *The Long Loneliness* (New York: Harper & Row, 1952), 134.

community. What I find humbling is that I've come to learn as much from the homies as I have from Father Greg—and he would agree. In Greg's book *Barking to the Choir*, he says, "We are at our healthiest when we are most situated in awe, and at our least healthy when we engage in judgment. . . . Standing at the margins with the broken reminds us not of our own superiority but of our own brokenness. Awe is the great leveler."[16] As I pushed myself to stand at the margins and learned to "open my eyes and heart," I learned a great deal about generosity, gratitude, and grace.

The Poor Are the Most Generous among Us

When I was growing up, on Sunday nights my father would sit at the kitchen table and pay all the bills that were due that week. Money was always tight, and very little was left over. If some was, my father would immediately put it into a passbook savings account at the local savings and loan. When he finished the bill paying, he would give us our allowances for the week. To get the allowance, we would informally report on the chores that were finished or not finished for that week. My siblings and I were pretty compliant and did most of our chores, so our allowance was usually paid in full. The allowance was two dollars per week—but one dollar was to be put into the church collection basket the following Sunday. My father instilled in us a sense of responsibility to help those less fortunate than ourselves. My friends would get an allowance that was much more than mine, and I knew they didn't give anything at church. So early in my life I saw a difference in what I was being taught and how it was to mold my life ahead: while we might not have much, what we do have should be shared.

As my career took off, my wife and I were able to donate more abundantly, and we felt good doing so. We became active in organizations our sons were participating in and felt a sense of responsibility to give back to those who helped our children along. In my mind, there was always a balance to take care of my family, ensure our future, and when available, donate to organizations

---

16. Gregory Boyle, *Barking to the Choir: The Power of Radical Kinship* (New York: Simon and Schuster, 2017), 54.

that help people. Fortunately, millions of Americans donate and have a proud tradition of giving back.

Being at Homeboy has enlightened me on what true generosity looks like. In fact, I've come to see that I'm really not that generous, which is a bit of an odd realization given that my wife and I have donated more than one million dollars to charities and people over the past twenty years. I'm nowhere near as charitable as the people I've come to work with: the poor, the demonized, the forgotten. I am amazed and humbled by the willingness of our folks to share whatever they have with others, for it comes straight from their hearts.

I witnessed this quickly within the first few weeks of being at Homeboy. As I was trying to understand the organization better, I would have lunch with as many folks as I could find. One time, I was out to lunch with Hector and realized that he almost never finished his meal, taking the remaining portion in a to-go box. On the walk back to the office, he'd walk across the street and seek out a homeless guy to whom he'd hand the other half of his lunch. Other times, Hector would bring his lunch back and would immediately seek out a new trainee and hand over his meal. Each time I saw Hector do this, I wondered why I don't and why those thoughts don't come naturally to many of us.

Most of our case managers and all our navigators have been clients of our program who have been promoted from within. While they perform the duties of their job, they also go above and beyond to help our trainees. In good times, when our trainees get into a financial bind, we as an organization can provide financial assistance or find a service agency to help. In bad times or when the money is needed right away, at an organizational level we are not always able to help. In such cases, I've witnessed our case managers and navigators reach into their own pockets—putting food on the table and diapers on babies, making restitution payments or child-support payments, or providing a safe place in a motel for a night so their client can avoid an abusive spouse. All good reasons. All in the name of the struggles the poor have when facing the tyranny of the diapers that the Forgotten America battles on a regular basis.

When I witness these selfless acts of charity and kinship, it makes me proud to be part of an organization that has this ethos. It also makes me wince, because I know that the people giving the money don't have much money of their own—regularly living paycheck to paycheck. Nevertheless, it makes me see firsthand how the "poor" have the most generous hearts.

I have been amazed and humbled by the willingness of our folks to share whatever they have with others. This comes straight from the heart. However, one could cynically (and often in a racist way) think that it's because "they don't know how to save money" and that they are spending their money with "no regard" or "they have no sense of money." Generosity is not just about simply giving money—it's about sharing what you have, offering to another person that which is precious to you.

Miguel is extraordinary in this way. He joined Homeboy Industries about four years ago, after being recently released from state prison, where he served eighteen years. He went in when he was seventeen years old. Not many people go into state prison at that age. Miguel came to Homeboy through the recommendation and the advice of one of the guys that used to be in his gang—who also happened to be a manager in our program. He felt so guilty about recruiting Miguel into the gang that he stuck with Miguel over the years. When Miguel got out of prison, the manager wanted to make sure Miguel came to Homeboy. It's a common phenomenon for folks to feel as if they are frozen in time after a long prison sentence, particularly if they go in as a young person. While their bodies are eighteen years older, often their minds are still much younger. Miguel soaked in what Homeboy had to offer, worked hard to move his life circumstances forward in a positive direction, and became good about helping other young guys transition into the program.

Miguel is a tall man, about six feet four inches, with a big, sturdy frame and a long ponytail. You can see why the gang would have wanted someone like Miguel—he looks like an intimidating force. His roots in Mexico go back to the indigenous people of the region. He strongly embraces Native American culture, practicing customs that involve sweat lodges and retreats out in the mountains. Ever since the first time I saw Miguel at Homeboy, I noticed he wore an ornate silver necklace of Native American design, a "medicine bag" given to him by his family. He was known to always wear that silver necklace.

Miguel is a guy who observes people, analyzes information quickly, and is situationally aware. All good skills to have in security. In fact, Miguel now leads our security team—one of the best security teams out there. These guys are all former clients and fairly solid in their recovery from gang addiction. They can see things that you or I just don't see. They notice things before they happen, fearlessly protect the people of Homeboy, and ensure that the "house" remains a sanctuary.

As a nonprofit, we receive a lot of donations, such as cash, equipment, and vehicles. When someone donates a car, we resist the urge to turn it into cash. Instead, we allow that car to be given away to one of our clients so that person doesn't have to take public transportation to get to Homeboy. Buses or the metro rail line regularly go through rival gang neighborhoods, which puts homies in a dangerous position. When we know someone is in this situation, we go out of our way to find them a vehicle. When people call us up and say they want to donate a car, we send two folks out to pick it up and bring it back. We get the paperwork done and write the donor a letter in deep gratitude.

About two years ago, a woman wanted to donate her car. She said she no longer had use for it. It was her daughter's car, and she had just passed away. We set up the appointment for our guys to pick it up. Miguel was one of those guys. Before he left, we let him know that this woman had just lost her daughter and asked him to keep this in mind when he spoke with her. Miguel is an engaging guy with a warm smile, who is always going to be friendly—no matter what. When they returned with the car, I happened to see Miguel downstairs and asked him, "How did that pick-up go?" He said, "Let me tell you a little about it." He said he sat and spoke with the woman for about forty-five minutes and learned that her daughter was killed just a few weeks earlier. Miguel said that she held no grievance or anger but was still visibly distraught. He could see her pain. So he took off his silver necklace—the one his family had given him, the one that has cultural significance to him—and handed it to this woman as a sign of care, kinship, compassion, and healing. The woman cried, knowing that she now had a prized possession of Miguel's. It meant a lot to them both.

When he told me that story, I was astounded by his generosity. I thought, *Would I give up a family possession like that to a stranger I'd just met? Would I have the openheartedness, the abundance to be there for that woman, to give her something that was so important to me?* Miguel, like many of our people, has that natural ability to live so generously. Our homies live simply, with no regrets, and they are here to help other people. There's no doubt Miguel was better off having an experience of kinship with that woman, as was she. Those examples of generosity should inspire us to do likewise.

Why are the poor so much more generous than the rest of society? Perhaps it's because they are not seeking money as their goal but rather are focused on living in the moment: becoming whole, healed, and being in community with others. I think they are just more spacious with their generosity, and in this way, I feel they are more in God's light. God gives with abundance; shouldn't we all? In the Christian teachings about money, many quote Luke 16:13: "You cannot serve God and wealth." Spiritual teacher Richard Rohr's point on this subject is that Jesus says we've eventually got to make a conscious choice here. We're wired to focus on short-term, practical gains. Yes, money does solve short-term problems, but I hear Jesus saying that the long-term solution is to seek relationships over money.

However, from my insights into the Forgotten America, I want to shout this: "Money *does* solve problems!" Just ask the mother skipping meals so that she can buy diapers, or ask the father who must choose to live with bad teeth so he can pay rent or keep the lights on. It's a cliché of the well-off to say, "Money doesn't solve anything"; they don't have to choose between food or diapers. The larger point here is that exquisite mutuality at the margins with the poor begins with openhearted kinship. Removing the barriers of the Forgotten America will fail if all we think about is the pursuit of money and we don't concurrently pursue the nonmaterial things, such as real relationships with people who live in the Forgotten America. The lives of all Americans will remain out of balance if we try to serve both God and money. Nothing good comes from a singular focus on money. The key is balance: each of us needs to figure out our greater purpose, our life's focus, our collective enjoyment of life, and our giving in this kind of abundance as our priority.

Our trainees and staff understand this at a gut level. The poor are less likely to pretend to be virtuous while the middle and upper classes skillfully disguise their problems behind a facade of self-righteousness. As our folks struggle to change their lives, struggle to heal, struggle to come to terms with their own self-doubt and errors—with the barriers of society—they surrender and don't prioritize the accumulation of wealth. They can find joy living simply in kinship with one another.

In the face of extreme poverty and a brutal life of trauma, they find pure joy in one another, in family, in their relationship with God, in a way that many of us can't. For sure, they want and need and deserve more money. They want their families to be healed, and they have many needs. They have no pretense. They are givers. Givers with generous hearts.

Community-Level Generosity

While the generosity of our trainees is so authentic and profound, the generosity of our donors allows our mission to endure. Homeboy has some terrific donors who are high on the spectrum of giving with abundance. I've had a chance to meet many of them, and they are incredibly wonderful people. Homeboy brings out the best in people. Many give to the organization with no expectation in return, other than to help those who are less fortunate. We are blessed to have many generous people who trust that we are good stewards of their money and will use it to facilitate turning people's lives around. Among the best donors are those who say, "Just use the money where you see fit, no need to report back specifically, no need to designate it to a particular area." They understand our mission and know the hardest funds to come by are those to support core operations.

We raise funds for many different areas of Homeboy: from tattoo removal to case management, from peer navigations to mental health, from substance abuse to domestic violence, from educational classes to work-skills training. For foundations that have a particular focus area, we can provide facts, figures, and outcomes in those designated areas. When we receive a sizable gift and it comes with a note saying, "We love your mission and work, please spend how you see fit," it makes me pause, and a tremendous feeling of gratitude washes over me—knowing how special that is. I tip my hat to those who give this way. It's a true sign of generous, openhearted giving, and it mirrors the generous giving our people do with one another. This type of giving brings everyone together in kinship and community.

Over the years, we've had many close encounters with financial stress. Philosophically, I've come to view these situations in two distinctly different ways. The first view is in the classical board-governance sense: the organization should not push the limit to nearly exhaust our financial resources to help so many people. I want to make clear here that I'm only talking about depleting the money in the bank, not borrowing money. We do not have continued long-term debt to cover operating expenses, and at the end of each fiscal year, we are debt-free. However, during the stressful times, we have come close to not making payroll. The classical view is that this type of financial performance is subpar and puts the organization in too much danger.

The second way to view this is the way I look at it now: pushing the limits is true to our mission. We are going to do everything possible to help as many people as possible. We are going to stretch every nickel today and count on money coming in the future so that it all works out. One way this works for Homeboy is that the largest part of our fundraising happens in the autumn, and the slowest part of the year is summer—when we are busiest. Often we enter the summer with very low reserves; if we took the classical approach, we would be required to cut payroll and stop bringing in clients who need help—holding back until the fall fundraising season begins. I now resist that approach. I break that rule and instead have faith that we will have a normal fundraising fall—that the money will be replenished.

The choice comes down to deciding whether to help forty more people for three months or hold off and have a better balance sheet. In general, board members and executives get judged on balance sheets, but the work we do is all about helping people. I've seen what happens when we turn people away: they keep gangbanging, keep dealing drugs, become more violent. Father Greg and I would rather take the financial risk, which brings with it outsiders' finger-wagging over our financial management. All of which makes those large, unexpected gifts that are unrestricted all the more special. I can't thank these people enough for their abundant generosity.

Gifts are crucial to supporting our mission, and we know we shouldn't be so reliant upon them. We have tried over the years to access more government dollars for the work we do. Los Angeles County spends a lot of money each year on education, mental health services, reentry services, and substance-abuse treatment efforts. These are areas in which we are exceptionally effective, as we have a unique cultural competency in the addictions of gang members and violent offenders. In fact, L.A. County's annual budget in these areas is more than thirty billion—*billion* with a capital *B*! We receive less than a million dollars per year from the county, and in some years we receive zero. Their reasoning is that they want to do it themselves and have no need for community-based organizations.

I knew we had to find a way to receive county money to take the stress off running the organization with just donor and business dollars. So I created a presentation to be used with elected officials, as we were soliciting financial support from them. It's easy to get meetings and lunches with elected officials. They very much appreciate what Homeboy does and stands for—and they greatly admire and respect Father Greg. In my presentation, I showed our recidivism rate of 30 percent against the statewide average of 70 percent. I showed them the number of people we serve and the cost savings we generate for the county, city, and state—to the tune of about ten million dollars annually. Compare that to an annual cost of $55,000 per individual (a low estimate) for the 100,000-plus adults incarcerated each year in California. It seemed obvious to me that Homeboy's annual return on public investment would be appealing to the county, saving them ten million annually while creating tremendous public value. It's mind boggling that the county wouldn't want to chip off a few million dollars from their annual budget of thirty *billion* dollars so that we could serve more gang members while reducing the overall incarceration rate and high cost of incarceration each year. But alas, my facts and figures weren't enough for them.

On one occasion, I had a Los Angeles council member tell me that it was an excellent presentation but he couldn't be persuaded any further until I had an economist endorse the savings amount. I was stunned. I had three numbers in my presentation that, when multiplied together, yielded the savings—each of those numbers was public information. Unless I could get an economist to put their name behind the multiplication of the three numbers, nothing was going to happen. Stall.

In addition to the incredible annual county budget of thirty-plus billion dollars, the L.A. Sheriff's Department has an additional annual budget of three-plus *billion* dollars. The sheriff's department proclaims that its Twin Towers Men's Central Jail is the largest mental health institution in the United States.[17] They have myriad challenges, particularly with a high rate of recidivism. Father Greg and I had a meeting with Sheriff Lee Baca, the longtime L.A. County sheriff who was a nationally recognized leader in the law-enforcement community—until he was convicted of conspiracy to obstruct justice, and of lying to federal prosecutors.[18] One day a few years ago, we had a breakfast meeting at Homegirl Café with him. He was respectful, courteous, and professional. After the pleasantries, I worked my way through a presentation about Homeboy's program, our successes, our singular impact on the safety of Los Angeles, and the ten-million-dollar savings. Sheriff Baca didn't say much during the presentation and in the end responded with his point of view. He said, "Tom, I appreciate all that Homeboy does, but in fact, we in the sheriff's department have all the same programs, and county money shouldn't be used to fund community-based organizations. You have your private donors and that is what you should focus on." In my mind, I'm thinking, *You provide the same programs in county jail?* He's deluded to think that their programs work. Father Greg has an expression: "You need to be free to choose to be free." Does Sheriff Baca really believe that inmates will open up to his officers about their trauma, about the sadness over the crimes they've committed? Of course, they attend his programs—they often have little choice in the

17. Los Angeles County Sheriff's Department, "Twin Towers Correctional Facility" (2014), http://shq.lasdnews.net/pages/tgen1.aspx?id=TTC.

18. Matt Hamilton, "Former Los Angeles County Sheriff Lee Baca Is Now a Prison Inmate in Texas," *Los Angeles Times* (February 5, 2020), https://www.latimes.com/california/story/2020-02-05/former-los-angeles-county-sheriff-lee-baca-is-now-a-prison-inmate-in-texas.

matter. The policy priorities of the government and their agencies are revealed in their spending of our public funds. Whom are they truly serving?

Society needs to invest in community-based programs that help people after they have been released, but Los Angeles city and county bureaucracy is more invested in keeping the dollars they see as theirs and deprioritizing the communities they serve. We need new policies and contracts that not only provide a return on public investment but also create effective and sustainable public services. We need to stop thinking that the same old policies that have been in place are making a difference. We need to stop leading from the top down with pronouncements and be willing to take risks on new approaches. Dismantling structural barriers that create racial inequality and inequity will provide a pathway out of poverty for individuals and organizations who already have the collective intelligence to create meaningful change. Until civil society holds its government officials accountable, organizations like Homeboy will need to depend on the generosity of their committed donors so that communities can heal and thrive.

Lessons about Gratitude at Homeboy

The lessons from the homies and the generosity of the community have led me to understand and experience gratitude at a much deeper level too. I think of the great number of people we serve—people who would otherwise be trapped in a vicious cycle of trauma or left for dead—and the generous support of thousands of donors each year. I firmly acknowledge the impact these gifts and givers have on Homeboy. The "Homeboy movement," as one generous donor calls it, is the action of a wide community creating meaningful and sustainable change in gratitude and the graceful appreciation of each other.

In his book *Putting on the Heart of Christ*, Gerald Fagin has a profound chapter on gratitude. Each time I read it, images and instances of Homeboy flash into my mind. I think about the generosity of the homies with one another. I think of the special gifts we have received from donors. I think about how my views on gifting have changed. I love when Fagin says, gratitude "is the movement within the human heart that goes beyond the gift to the giver."[19] At Homeboy, when we receive gifts, our thoughts go to the giver.

While in community with one another, gifts are offered, and our hearts are moved by being in kinship with the giver. When Miguel gave his necklace to the woman to heal her sadness, that was truly a movement of the heart toward kinship. In our community of homies, gratitude is practiced and recognized.

Fagin's other line also resonates with me a great deal: "Grateful people do not claim things as their own, but cherish everything as given and received."[20] As we give with openhearted abundance, we are clearly realizing what each of us has. We see the human value of one another, a gift as well to be shared. When donors give so generously, they are affirming that they are grateful and seek to share with others. When Hector hands over his food to the guy on the street, he is cherishing what he has received and pays it forward.

Last, Fagin says, "Gratitude does not turn us inward with a sense of passive contentment but points us outward in service."[21] As our homies move through our programming, as they transform their lives through healing, they move from being inwardly focused and now look to help others.

Psychologist Charles Shelton says of gratitude that "it enriches love because it enables a person to break out of the role of victim and work toward healing. It counteracts the human tendency to focus on the negative rather than on the positive."[22] Fagin says, "Gratitude expands our hearts and opens them to the richness and the giftedness of life. It fosters self-esteem, positive relationships of trust, and leads to joy that encourages sharing of one's gifts."[23] These two thoughts by Shelton and Fagin sum up the theory of action that occurs at Homeboy. Move from victim to healing—fostering positive self-esteem. Every day our people practice these concepts to their fullest. They make the choice to be grateful. As they talk openly about their own gratitude, it becomes infectious—and a strong part of the organization's culture. For me—like others—being part of this community has pulled me along to see life in a much more grateful way.

---

19. Gerald M. Fagin, *Putting on the Heart of Christ: How the Spiritual Exercises Invite us to a Virtuous Life* (Chicago: Loyola Press, 2010), 35.

20. Fagin, *Putting on the Heart of Christ*, 29.

21. Ibid., 37–38.

22. Ibid., 37.

23. Ibid., 37.

As I reflect about my own journey, I feel as if I've always appreciated what I have, but it took me so long to better understand what true gratitude means. My guess is that many other people are similarly appreciative, but I see now that true gratitude moves beyond appreciation. When we embrace gratitude, our hearts fill with thanksgiving, and we see the world as a gift. And we recognize the true givers: those people on the margins of the Forgotten America.

Be Available for Moments of Grace

The people here have taught me to look for moments of grace. Through my "Homeboy-hued eyes," I can see these instances, and they lead me to experience life more wholly. Grace is the pot of gold at the end of the rainbow made from generosity and gratitude. As you become more generous with an open heart, you can be grateful for the gifts received. For the giver, the "payoff" is the moments of grace that open up to you. Drinking in these moments of grace makes you want to become more generous and grateful. A beautiful circle.

I would never have experienced these moments of grace—or, as others call them, "God moments"—if it were not for being in this unique community. These moments sneak up on you, and sometimes you see them only upon reflection.

This is the story of Demetrius. Every Thursday at Homeboy, we have what's called the selection committee. This is where we choose who becomes part of our paid employment program. To qualify for the selection committee, you need to test drug-free, attend our orientation program, have been a gang member, and have been incarcerated. Most important, you must want to change your life around. I do my best to participate in the weekly selection committee interviews. One such Thursday about six months ago, an African American man in his late thirties came in. He had just gotten out of prison two weeks earlier, and a friend of his told him he should come to Homeboy Industries. Demetrius did a long prison stint—about eight years. In fact, he had been incarcerated multiple times.

In the selection committee we look for people who really need us the most. As Father Greg says, "We reverse cherry-pick." We pick the people who we know are the hardest cases, those least likely to succeed. If we don't help them, no one else will, and they'll be back on the streets, running with the gang, doing crime, recidivating back into jail. In the selection committee interviews, we ask questions relating to background history, such as where they live, what gang they're with, whether they have an ID, and if they have a high school diploma. We also ask questions about their readiness to change. I asked Demetrius, "Why do you want to join Homeboy?" He looked up at me and he said, "I'm just tired of this life. It's been nothing but problems for me. My father was in a gang, my uncles were in a gang. I just want to stop. I just want a different life."

At that point, I knew he was right for our program and that we could help him. Demetrius then went on to talk about some of the dreams and aspirations he had. He wanted to get a regular job; he wanted to earn legitimate money; but he knew he couldn't get a job with his felony record and his lack of work experience. He knew he needed to work on his parenting skills, his anger-management skills, and most important, he knew he needed to stay away from the gang.

When we get folks right out of prison, they often juggle two competing forces. It's cliché to call them forces of good and forces of evil, but I see it kind of like that. Deep down, an individual knows they want to change their life, particularly as they're thinking about getting out and being released. They walk through our doors not knowing how to change, but they know we're here to help them. We hold up a mirror so they can see their God-given goodness, to let them anchor themselves in their goodness as they work to heal. We also know that when they leave our doors—their sanctuary—at the end of the day, they go back into their neighborhood. They go back to a place of bad influences, a place where people say, "You are one of us, let's go out, we are your family."

We concentrate on holding people as closely as we can and make it clear that there's goodness in each person—and that each person can change, no matter their background. Demetrius, for some reason, struck me as unique. He had a spark of desire, a sparkle in his eye. He had charisma and a gift of gab. He also had a lot of pain, and he wanted to work through it. Over the next two months, while he was in our program, he worked on himself. It wasn't always a straight line. There was a time when we had to ask him to step away from our program because he had tested positive for drugs. That's a sign for us that people aren't ready to do the hard work. We always say, "We're your family, we're here for you. When you're ready, come back."

Demetrius came back. He was building relationships, making a difference, changing his life. Then, two months into working at Homeboy, he was out with his friends on a Friday night. He was at a spot he shouldn't have been, at a party he should have avoided—and he was gunned down by a rival gang as he was leaving the house. Shot in the head. The next morning, some of our team members went to the hospital to be by his side. He was brain-dead at the time. They were waiting for his family to come take him off life support. A day later, he passed away.

Demetrius had an impact on all of us. I know that every one of our trainees felt the pain of what happened because the loss of Demetrius triggered the trauma of dozens of other, similar losses within our community. Homies who were doing well in their new lives gunned down in a moment, just because they put themselves in the wrong spot at the wrong time. They must remain vigilant at all times. The amount of energy that requires must be incalculable.

What also impacts his story is that we have former Bloods, Crips, and Mexican gang members throughout our organization. To say these gangs do not get along on the outside is a gross understatement. What was remarkable was that the Homeboy folks who showed up at the hospital transcended the racial divide and their former gang affiliations. That's not unusual for us but is highly unusual for hospital personnel. As the funeral was being planned, we wanted to make sure we represented Demetrius—represented all that Homeboy stands for.

About thirty of us went to his funeral services. It was in South Central Los Angeles. I had never been to that section of town, to this type of church and funeral hall. Because of the gang-related nature of the killing, the situation was full of tension. Essentially, the funeral was being held in his rival gang's territory—that same rival gang who shot him dead. There were police outside, making sure things went smoothly. There were probably five hundred people at the service. Our Homeboy group pretty much sat in the back row. Of the five hundred people in attendance, all were African American except for half of our group who were Hispanic and the two of us who were white—I was the only white man in the congregation. We sat in the back row and respectfully said our prayers and participated in the service.

This was the first time I'd attended a funeral in an African American tradition. The ministers led off with a lot of prayer and spoke for approximately twenty minutes on the teachings of Jesus. A lot of music and singing were incorporated throughout the service—it truly felt like a celebration of Demetrius's life. From where I sat, I could see a lot of tears; the pain of losing Demetrius was evident in the body language of the people gathered there. After the ministers finished, a dozen people came up and gave eulogies. This went on for a long time. Each person spoke about Demetrius. Everything they said made me feel sadder and more joyous at the same time. They talked about Demetrius and how they saw him. They talked about the women in his life, the womanizing he did. They talked about the cars he drove and the clothes he wore. They talked about his uncles in the gang—his uncles who are incarcerated—and about his homies being their friends. Essentially, while they were glorifying him, they were glorifying the life of a gang member.

What made me sad was that this was not the Demetrius we knew at Homeboy in those two months that he was with us. He was happy with who he was. We saw the joyousness of it, we saw him seeking his goodness, not running with the gang, not spinning stories, not womanizing, not drinking. We saw the goodness of who he was. Speaking with Father Greg afterward, I realized that for the two months Demetrius was with us, he found his spirituality and relationship with God. Part of me is joyous that we got to experience that, but part of me is sad that his family and friends never did. One man came up several times to facilitate eulogies from incarcerated people in jail—from Florida to California. He placed the cell phones to the mic, and as they talked about Demetrius, I realized they didn't know him—at least not in the way we knew him in those last two months of his life at Homeboy. In this environment of eulogy and remembering Demetrius's life, I felt a moment of grace upon us. We got to see how Homeboy provided such a stark and wonderful contrast to the old world Demetrius had belonged to. We got to see Demetrius find who he was, at least for a few weeks. He will always be a part of our lives.

There is also the story of Shirley, one of our senior executives. One day, she and a case manager went to the apartment of a former trainee who had just come home from the hospital. This trainee had been beaten so badly she was unrecognizable. She was frightened, despondent, and in pain. Shirley shared her experience of grace that permeated the room during this time of kinship in the small community of these three women. No longer were they a senior executive, a case manager, and a trainee; they were but three women sharing with each other a common understanding of pain—while finding strength together.

Over the years I've had the pleasure of giving annual merit raises to many employees. I think one of the most enjoyable times for managers is when they can provide a substantial raise in pay to a valued employee. I feel a bit guilty because it's not my money I'm giving away—it's Homeboy's money. However, it is money the individual has earned. I feel guilty for feeling so good about just being the messenger. That being said, it is hugely endearing to give a raise or promotion to a former client, a homie. They are beyond grateful. They are emotional, they are stunned, and usually they feel as if they don't deserve it. Overall, they are overcome with emotion in realizing that they are valued, validated, and seen—because at no other time in their life has this happened to them. To be a part of their joyous realization that they matter and that people truly care about them is—certainly for me—a moment of grace, a gift.

Generosity and gratitude are personal sets of choices that allow for grace-filled experiences with one another and with God. Being at Homeboy has allowed me to gain greater insight, knowledge, and practice around these concepts. But like most of my learnings from Homeboy, I sometimes struggle with how to bring this type of purpose into the rest of my life. It's much easier to be one's "best self" in the Homeboy community, but when we are around others who are not so generous and grateful, how do we maintain it? How does one stay on the grateful path? Most of us spend our days at work, completing tasks for others. What choices are we making to show our appreciation and gratitude, not only at work but in our personal lives too?

I've come to understand that we shouldn't always expect our professional lives to be the definition of who we are and how we think about the rest of life. Often, business is just business. We go to work; we understand our role and fulfill it to the best of our ability. We are kind to our coworkers, and that's it. Before coming to Homeboy, I felt that the nonprofessional part of my life was more important and a better measure of how to view myself. Since being here, doing business differently includes being true to myself at all times. If I strive for generosity, gratitude, and grace, I should offer them throughout the day to my coworkers, even if it's not reciprocated.

Well-run companies are those that are people-oriented and have a culture of positive engagement. This hallmark is visible when employees pull together in the same direction, when they care for one another and support the collective work effort. These all touch on the practice of generosity and gratitude that leads to moments of grace in the business environment.

I was spending a great deal of my effort to understand generosity, gratitude, and grace at a far deeper level. I knew that my life until this point was charmed and "giving," but I look back now and see just how superficial my understanding was. My purpose and motivation weren't very deep at all. Without Homeboy opening my eyes to the true meaning of these concepts, I think I'd still be on the surface of these practices: going to fundraising galas and feeling good about my contributions but never getting into the true meaning. I could honestly say that I had never appreciated the graceful moments I had experienced—such a shame. However, now I was opening my heart to allow them in.

And I was asking important questions: *What choices am I making in my personal life, within my personal relationships, to be available for moments of grace? To be more generous and grateful? To be my true self at all times? To experience the present moment, in kinship, with everyone? For it can't always be about planning for the future. It's also about being present with the person who is sitting in front of me. Perhaps for the one who walks through the door and literally has no options and needs help. Giving generosity of time, of heart, and of resources might just help keep this person's life from spiraling down even further.*

Gratitude and an Obligation

I had sincere gratitude. I still do.

I believe that Homeboy exists only because of the time, talent, and treasure it receives from so many people. I have such sincere gratitude for these generous individuals who are part of the broader Homeboy community. Because of this I feel a sense of obligation to them and to Father Greg. I also have a great deal of gratitude for a management team who knows how to help people transform their lives.

As I learned about gratitude, I saw it as my job to make sure Homeboy kept going. Which meant that I needed to find them more money and to find the path for long-term sustainability.

We had made all the business changes we needed to be efficient. There was no more "fat." We couldn't save our way to helping more people. The issue was still too many people coming in needing our help—which depleted all our resources.

At this time, I saw the strain and stress on Greg more often. I wondered how much longer he could keep this up. I also knew that he wouldn't give up, and I knew that the organization needed to learn how to thrive without Greg and me. We needed to develop the next generation of leaders while finding long-term financial resources.

I knew that the culture of a loose organizational structure and sporadic individual accountability would be the issues that held back organizational growth. The harder question was: How could we make the shift while maintaining the aspects of the culture that made this place so magical?

CHAPTER 7

MERITOCRACY DOES NOT ALWAYS WORK

Those who do manage to find their way to us have likely heard about Homeboy on the streets or in jail. They are courageous to step through our doors for the first time and simply ask for help. Our social capital provides enough proof to them that transformation is possible and does happen here—which in turn allows them to be open-minded about our program. One of the key questions during the intake-interview process relates to their readiness to give up gang life. It's not unusual to hear hesitation in their voices. Even though the gang "did them wrong," they still have a sense of loyalty, affinity, and identity with the gang. For many, their entire family—mother, father, siblings, children—are all gang members. They fear giving up the gang because no one will be there for them. Our answer is that the Homeboy community is here and always will be. But right at the beginning, it's hard for them to see and trust that. Inevitably, trainees come into our program with one foot in the Homeboy sanctuary and one foot in their old neighborhood.

As homies leave jail or prison and come into Homeboy for help, one can almost see an angel on one shoulder saying, "Go to Homeboy, take care of yourself for the first time in your life. Be an example of a good parent; God believes in you." Meanwhile, on the other shoulder the devil is whispering, "No one is ever going to help you. You've been a nothing your whole life; the gang is the only family you have. You don't deserve to have good things happen to you." There is a real battle going on for their soul. We realize this and start by simply offering some concrete help to begin building a healthy and positive relationship with them. We also know that when they leave our building and go home for the night, more than likely "home" will be in their gang neighborhood, where they are exposed to multiple negative influences that might be irresistible.

I have seen that each and every person who is looking to be in our program has the desire to "do good," "to be better," to be the person they are meant to be. The struggle is that they don't know how to make this transition on their own, and the structural barriers that exist are insurmountable for most, regardless of how hard they work. When homies come into our eighteen-month therapeutic community program, they do not immediately enter as a trainee in one of our social enterprise businesses. Before work therapy begins, a whole team of talented and dedicated professionals surrounds them—literally and figuratively—initiating the positive bonds and emotional support that will enable his or her individualized recovery, development plan, and, through exquisite mutuality, their transformation.

Currently we have only enough resources to select one new trainee each week out of a pool of more than two hundred community clients we may have at any given time. When I first began serving on the selection committee and participating in interviews, I wondered, *How do we pick one out of so many applicants?* How do we go about choosing what for many might mean the difference between life and death? Do we take the one who deserves it more? Do we take the one who is more worthy? Do we take the one who is the most likely to succeed? Do we take the one who will work the hardest? Should we use a measurement scale for each applicant and figure out what profile best succeeds and use this scoring to pick among the many applicants fighting for their lives? The answer to these questions reveals the essence of Homeboy's philosophy, and it runs counter to the notion of meritocracy and other concepts behind the American Dream.

However, before we get there, it's important to understand the external forces (one might even characterize them as structural forces) that exert power on our internal decision-making processes. Homeboy is blessed to have many generous donors, many of them large grant-making foundations. Of the prerequisites for funding from the foundation world, one is a measurement of results: a quantification of program outcomes as "proof of the success of the program." All these measurements make sense from a foundation perspective because they are trying to figure out who to fund and where their funds might have the greatest impact. Unfortunately, this dynamic not only creates competition among nonprofits but also steers how programs are designed to enable the most statistically significant results. This puts Homeboy in a rather unique and difficult position.

Reverse Cherry-Picking

It's Father Greg's perspective—based on decades of successfully facilitating thousands of transformations—that we "serve the hardest of the hardest cases." We are to serve those *least likely to succeed*, those no other county agency or nonprofit would touch. We dare to serve the seriously violent felons who are gang members. We serve the population that society responds to with, "Lock 'em up and throw away the key." But society is slowly learning that the Homeboy way of kinship, love, and respect makes a massive impact and produces unparalleled results. We are living proof that everyone is better than the worst thing they have ever done and that there is goodness in everyone. But because the demand is so great for our program and funding so scarce, we know that we need to show our work in a way our donors and government agencies prefer. So we keep track of our efforts statistically in two main metrics: successful trainee outcomes and business performance.

Several years ago, an independently funded two-year study of the Homeboy program found that 70 percent of the people participating in the program did not recidivate back into the jail or prison system on new charges. This compares extremely favorably to the statewide average of 30 percent nonrecidivism rate among other "similar" programs, who work mostly with offenders of *nonviolent* drug crimes. Our program's effective rate is more than two times the norm, and in contrast, we work mostly with violent felons. We work with the "hardest of the hardest cases," *and* we have grown to become the largest and most successful therapeutic gang-recovery program—and model—in the world. If we were measured on merit, we would be one of the most funded organizations in the nation. Sadly, the concept of meritocracy so common in our country's culture ends at our front doors.

So I return to my previous question: how does one go about choosing what for many might mean the difference between life and death? When I posed this question to Father Greg during one of my first selection committee meetings, he said, "What we do is 'reverse cherry-pick'; that is, we take the applicants who need it the most." He continued, "We don't take the ones that Homeboy needs the most to improve our statistics. We help those who ask us for help, without worrying about whether or not they will make our numbers look good."

While this sounds easy to say and to preach, when you are looking into the eyes of someone who's been in prison for twenty years for heinous crimes, it can be difficult at first not to judge that person by the worst thing he or she has ever done. However, this stance is a real motivator for our selection committee—many of them have been judged and defined this way their whole life. They know we are being authentic to our mission and that the transformative power of the program and community are very real. They've come to care about helping the person who is standing in front of them in the present moment, with little regard for "getting in trouble" for helping someone who might fail and give us a bad statistic—or bad press for that matter.

There is a big *but* to this. A 70 percent "success rate" means we have a 30 percent "fail rate." On a few occasions, that fail rate can be both troubling and heartbreaking. We can happily talk for hours about the thousands of folks who have transformed their lives through our program, but the ones we've lost are seared into our hearts. To date, Father Greg says he has buried 244 gang members. Some were working hard on changing their lives but by simply being in the wrong place at the wrong time—visiting a parent or childhood friend in the old neighborhood—lost everything. Other times, lives are lost when homies drop out of our program; they often return to the gang and eventually prison, leaving carnage in their wake.

One such example is a former gang member named DeShawn, an African American man in his late twenties. DeShawn came to us pretty much straight from prison and was active in our program. He embraced the role of a vocal leader, a passion that led him to become engaged in our local community-organizing group. We sent him to Sacramento to learn more about organizing and how to make one's voice heard. He spoke often about Homeboy and the issues that mattered to him. We considered him an emerging leader. However, six months into his time with us, he started to become less engaged, and we were having trouble reaching him. The one rule we have at Homeboy is that if you are not working on yourself, you leave the program and come back when you are ready. This was the situation with DeShawn. Even though he was no longer "officially" in our program, we still cared for him, and the team kept trying to reach out to him. Then one weekend, we learned that he had been arrested for an assassination-like murder of a woman. Poof, just like that, his life and identity were forever changed back to that of a violent criminal, and he was incarcerated for a long term. Our hearts broke for his victims and our hearts broke for DeShawn.

When the news hit the newspapers, it was reported that he was part of the Homeboy program. As a follow-up to the first story, the newspaper reached out to us for comment. Naturally, this type of negative press had us worrying about our donor base and how they might react—we couldn't afford to lose a penny, because that would mean "downsizing," and homies who weren't ready to leave Homeboy would have to. Coincidently during this time, a board member paid for Homeboy to retain a PR firm that had a crisis-management communications team in their New York office. Naturally, we attempted to tap into this new resource. They declined. To this day, I don't know the exact reasons they backed out of helping us. Perhaps it was because this story was "too hot" and they feared it might tarnish their reputation.

The reporter asked us for an official comment. We could have easily distanced ourselves from DeShawn and said he was no longer part of our program, that he had "failed our program," or simply just expressed our sympathies for the victims. In the end, through Father Greg's direction, we didn't make an official comment. We were not going to demonize DeShawn, nor were we going to feed into the notion that some people are just evil. We stand for all people, no matter what.

Father Greg is authentic, even when it goes against conventional wisdom and may hurt us economically. He will never demonize anyone, especially not someone who's had an awful life like that of DeShawn. I am willing to bet that no other organization would ever invest in the DeShawns of the world as we do. Government agencies find ways to "slow walk" such applications so that they don't have to help. Other nonprofits wouldn't take them on because of their high likelihood of failing and thereby hurting the organization's numbers. Homeboy stands for everyone, and that is what makes the organization so unique. This concept of standing with everyone and in particular the most despised, stands in stark contrast to how the rest of the world views people: through a merit-based system of measuring up, of bootstrapping yourself into becoming somebody via the "old-fashioned work ethic."

The Limits of a Merit-Based System

The Privileged America, the one I grew up in, is the America that meritocracy fits best. The Privileged America can live by the belief that a merit-based system has rules that create a level playing field. There is a quid pro quo: if you work harder than the rest and are smart, you will thrive in a world that has meritocracy-based values. People know what is expected, and if you achieve something, everyone else understands why it happened. The result came through your own merit and had nothing to do with playing favorites or tearing others down.

I believe that meritocracy even works to the benefit of those in the lower-middle-class world, especially first- and second-generation Americans. When your goal is to improve your status in life, it's easier when you know the rules of the game. How many times have we heard the Horatio Alger "rags to riches" type stories? The immigrant comes to America and makes a better life for himself and his family. This could be done only in a society that values and rewards hard work and fortitude.

I was raised in a middle-class Italian family in New Jersey, and we operated in this system of meritocracy. I was taught that I could achieve my American Dream through my hard work and ability. Indeed, I achieved successes big and small. For most of my adult life, I believed that my success had nothing to do with the station of life I was born into or whom I knew, for my family was not "connected." To put it into economic terms, through my own talent, hard work, and ability, I believed I was able to earn a decent living. I believed that over time, these rewards propelled me up the ladder, earning a spot in a higher socioeconomic class. I believed that everyone was given a fair shot, independent of their backgrounds, to do the same thing.

But I've come to see that this is not the reality for many people. Meritocracy doesn't work so well in the Forgotten America that our clients live in. Upon coming to Homeboy, I was a full-throated American Dream and meritocracy believer—before I learned a few humbling lessons. Father Greg once asked me, "Is meritocracy a worthiness code?" His question gave me pause. The $6MDM inside me held fast. After all, how might I otherwise explain and connect all my hard work and sacrifices with the riches and fruits of my labor? Father Greg went on, "The ego thrives on success, but the soul finds vitality in meaning. That's what we do at Homeboy. Success can be a by-product of our effort as well, but the emphasis is different here." We help people with *meaning*.

I saw several examples that tangibly challenged me to think differently about meritocracy. We had several managers who, if they were from the side of the tracks I was from, would be zooming up the ladder of success. But because they were not, life doesn't work out that way for them.

Carlos was a leader in our bakery, a man of much talent and ability. He lived in a run-down, rat-infested duplex; it was the only type of place he could get because his landlord looked past his criminal record and debts. Carlos paid his rent on time. He paid enough for what should have been a better place, but the system wouldn't let him in the front door—nor did it hold his slumlord accountable to maintain safe housing. Then there is another Homeboy leader, David, who would like to move his sons to a different school. But the school makes it known that they don't want parents who have been gang members. Clarence is an up-and-coming manager with lots of talent, and he's willing to work for what he earns. But without Homeboy giving him a higher-paying job, he would be toiling at minimum wage—while providing the same value somewhere else. I've seen a lot of folks who, given who they are today, in a true merit-based society would be earning a great deal more money based on their work ethic, abilities, and results. Not everyone had the same "fair shot" I had.

At Homeboy, we do not believe in a merit-based system. In fact, we are an antimeritocracy organization with an antimerit promotion system. The business world will say to someone looking for a promotion, "Before you get the promotion, you need to take on these responsibilities and demonstrate that you can do the job." People understand this dynamic and willingly put forth the effort because they trust they will get the promotion in a merit-based environment. This doesn't work in the Homeboy world. The people with lived experience who are in our program and businesses are not going to "move an inch" or "take on more work" until they get that promotion with a raise upfront. In a very antimeritocracy way, they don't trust that if they work hard, a payoff will come. They've had too many experiences of being lied to, talked down to, and given false commitments—by bureaucracies and management teams of authority figures (mostly white guys) who never really followed through in ways to make their workers' lives any better.

It took me a long time to figure this out. I still don't know if it's "right," but that is the way I've come to understand the forces at play. Now I look for the people with potential for advancement and promote them with raises without first insisting on proof that they can do the job. The key is to have a strong sense of their skills and talents and put them in the right job to ensure their success. This approach should not be conflated with saying, "He is a good person who understands the mission well, so let's promote him." You need to look for an emerging skill set that matches the needs for the job. Last, I tell them clearly, "Here's what I'm expecting out of you," and most of the time they step up and do the job. Some of my staff who have worked in the outside world's merit-based system are frustrated at me for operating this way. They feel that they have worked hard to prove themselves, and they see these early promotions of others as unfair. I understand their point of view, but I've seen it this way for many years now and know that we as a society need to think differently to drive for racial and social equality and equity.

In a broader sense, meritocracy has come under attack lately, and I'm in agreement—and have added a nuance. This line of thinking is best explained by Yale law professor Daniel Markovits in his book *The Meritocracy Trap: How America's Foundational Myth Feeds Inequality, Dismantles the Middle Class, and*

Devours the Elite.[24] He proposes that meritocracy is a way for the upper ends of society to hold on to what they have, to ensure that their children have a promising future. I agree that our current meritocracy enables the elites to keep their status for themselves and their families. I agree that passing along privileges of the elites to succeeding generations will keep only a certain stratum of people in that category. Markovits goes on to say that in the 1960s and 1970s, meritocracy broke the mold of the old "leisure class" and that hard work and acquiring certain skills enabled the people on the next rung down to propel themselves into the super elites. Once there, they become part of a rigged system that ensures their long-term status at the exclusion of others. Markovits's book is a wake-up call to the elites, written *by an elite* to shine a light on the hypocrisy of the elites touting the concept of the American Dream (for elites).

After reading Paulo Freire's *Pedagogy of the Oppressed*, I think that what Freire would say about meritocracy is that the oppressors work hard to keep the oppressed in their station in life, and thus the concept of the American Dream is a myth that keeps the oppressed placated. That the barriers the oppressors put in place for the oppressed are the antithesis of a meritocracy.

I understand why Americans hold dear to their hearts the concept of the American Dream and bitterly fight those who deny that it exists or suggest that it's a bad thing. However, the American Dream doesn't exist for those in the Forgotten America. In particular, the central theme of "hard work and dedication to an endeavor" is an overemphasized value when the people from the Privileged America look at those from the Forgotten America and can't figure out why they are having difficulty. They go so far as to accuse people of being lazy, not caring, or being good-for-nothings. Freire's position is that the elite, or privileged, feel entitled to their position. The oppressor is angered by what he sees as the oppressed's "ingratitude" for the "generosity" shown to them.

In the Forgotten America, that of the poor and disenfranchised, they have almost no chance in a merit-based situation. Over fifty years ago, Martin Luther King Jr. said, "I believe we ought to do all we can and seek to lift

---

24. Daniel Markovits, *The Meritocracy Trap: How America's Foundational Myth Feeds Inequality, Dismantles the Middle Class, and Devours the Elite* (New York: Penguin Press, 2019).

ourselves by our own bootstraps, but it is cruel jest to say to a bootless man that he ought to lift himself by his own bootstraps."[25] They cannot "boot strap" themselves up—they have no bootstraps to begin with! They have so many cultural and societal barriers that prevent them from even being able to play the game. Barriers such as no access to a good education, history of childhood trauma, no family network to fall back upon, insufficient financial resources, poor healthcare, and punishments in perpetuity as felons even though debts to society have been paid: felons can't vote, can't get federal loans, and face severe prejudice when trying to get a job or get their kids into a good school.

I agree with those who criticize our society's concept of meritocracy as being esoteric, conceptual, and aspirational at best, for those in the Privileged America. I agree that the reality of our system of meritocracy does not work well in enabling those from the lower socioeconomic strata to access the upper strata, and that as a result, society is not working so well. However, let's not throw out the baby with the bathwater. My view is that meritocracy does exist for the many rungs of our society's middle class but stops at the door of the poor.

The extreme position of meritocracy being "all bad" or "all good" misses what meritocracy means for the middle of society—the middle, wherein one is not extremely poor or oppressed, or a one percenter holding on tight to what one has. For people in the middle who want to improve their situation, do better for their children, and feel a sense of accomplishment, aspects of meritocracy do help them. There is no other system that allows this mobility or advancement in such a clearly understood way. From the standpoint of how a person can make her or his individual life better, a meritocracy is far superior to any other system. To me this has been the silver lining to the concept of the American Dream experience. We still have a system in place to move up the socioeconomic ladder. It does not enable the poor to get to the middle or the middle to get to the very top, but it is a good governing principle for those in the middle looking to improve their station in life.

---

25. Martin Luther King Jr., interview by Sander Vanocur, *NBC News*, May 8, 1967.

Last and important, a huge weakness of meritocracy is that it needs measurement and data. At Homeboy, we focus on our people believing in themselves, discovering God's love for them, and finding joy as a path forward. That is what we prize, and so we do not operate on a merit-based system. Someone doesn't transform their own life "better or sooner" than someone else. Finding one's worth is not a metric—there is no way to calculate that. There is no way to measure a person discovering his or her God-given goodness. Our clients can't and shouldn't be measured, for once you start measuring, you imply that some folks are not worth as much as others and that some folks just don't measure up, period.

While we decline to measure people and refuse to judge their worthiness, it's also proper to understand that workplace achievements help people grow as well. With earning more money comes more responsibility, which is reaffirming. Being promoted brings about a greater sense of self-worth and pride. In a spiritual sense, being measured by money is a nonstarter, but earnings tied to one's own work is a powerful thing for a sense of self.

The leadership development path forward for Homeboy will be one of walking that fine line of knowing that our trainees should not be measured and evaluated—and yet, when they become members of the management team, they need to understand that we all become dependent on their performance. We can't shy away from some level of accountability and merit-based systems, but we mustn't overemphasize it, for that will seep in and negatively impact our adherence to the mission. I've seen with my own eyes that when the mindset switch is made to focus on doing their job well, the sky's the limit for their career.

I think people need to understand that meritocracy does not apply to all aspects of life. Most of us live in two spheres of existence: our professional life and our life outside of work. Really, there is just our whole life. Our professional life generally exists in the business world, where there are a set of agreed-upon rules of operation. All types of "rules of thumb" and "dos and don'ts"—who's in charge, who you listen to, when you can disagree, when you can't, when to inform your supervisor—workplace rules, workplace habits, and so on. Typically, it's within the workplace that meritocracy should be active. It's not realistic to say that we're never going to rate someone's performance in terms of evaluating whether they're doing their job or not. It's okay to grade someone's performance on their job. That doesn't mean we're declaring them a good person or a bad person. The more people can understand and accept this sometimes-conflicting dichotomy, the better off we're going to be. We can't just take this measuring-up methodology and apply it to everybody and all aspects of life outside the workplace.

In God's eyes, we're all human beings, and we all have God's love in us. My God's love is not any better than your God's love. There's no judging or measuring. When Greg and others of his ilk say, "Let's not try to measure people, let's not try to size them up, don't judge them," it's about this. We're all in this greater community in which we don't presume to measure one another's goodness or worth.

Ultimately, the goal is to create a workplace culture where one can thrive. As Father Greg says, "Achievements are a by-product of thriving." Our efforts focus on providing an atmosphere in which people flourish and blossom so that they find their own worth. Imagine a society that collectively pursues and reaches the goal of having thriving workplaces. This is when we can do away with meritocracy and simply celebrate achievements.

When we're on the front lines working with our clients, we must remember that what's important for them is to heal and to discover that they have God's love too. They're not rotten or disposable, which is how society tends to see them. To Greg's point and others': once society understands that these people are just like the rest of us in terms of innate goodness, society will realize that it was wrong to have forever judged and marginalized them. Our trainees are working on the invisible processes of healing, gaining resilience, and creating community. The part of society that hangs on to the notion of meritocracy for all, that keeps trying to enforce a measurement protocol, is looking at it the wrong way. Nothing is gained by imposing a merit-based system on people who have already been severely disadvantaged by the system.

Not only are our folks in the same community as we are, as we move to kinship with the poor, we have the opportunity to learn something for ourselves. In Jesus' Sermon on the Mount, he teaches that "the meek will inherit the earth." I've always struggled with the meaning and implication of this concept. What does that really mean? Are the poor more special? Should I *work* to become poor and docile? The more I learn and think about it, I believe the lesson is to *live* meekly—that is, in humility. God's love is more apparent precisely because when we open our eyes and our hearts, we become more willing to let everything go and not worry about measuring up. The ego becomes deflated, and we experience God in a much fuller way—and more quickly than when we are worrying about the measurement of things. When people talk about spending time with the poor to see God, that's what I believe they are searching for. If you're stuck on measuring worth, consider this: "The ego thrives on success, but the soul finds vitality in meaning."

CHAPTER 8

JOY IS FOUNDATIONAL TO A THRIVING WORKPLACE

I was the $6MDM—a true and trained apparatus of corporate America. I was to be among the best at what it produced. Yet I knew I was missing one aspect of "the package" to make my way to the very, very top: a killer instinct. That instinct to trample over others to get there, to reach the top rung on the ladder. I decided that I was not going to get there at the expense of others. I could have done more to toot my own horn, to play hardball politics, but I felt my work and results alone should be rewarded. I'm good with the choices I made, for I received the gifts of time and freedom from the corporate world—both of which I know are gifts others don't often get. I wanted to do something of my own to help, and Homeboy gave me that opportunity. But what I quickly realized was that to do something that matters, it couldn't be about me; it had to be about others, through others. As Archbishop Desmond Tutu said, "Ultimately, our greatest joy is when we seek to do good for others." So, I put my head down and started working.

Upon becoming CEO at Homeboy, I was able to change the course of our financials. We now have had eight consecutive years of positive operating income, and our top-line revenue has grown from eleven million to thirty million dollars. While our financial numbers look good and over this time span we have helped more than forty thousand people from the community we serve, it was not always easy keeping the ship afloat, and most of the time I had to dig deep into my faith and motivation to keep going.

Each year is like performing a high-wire act all over again. We need to raise more than twenty million dollars, and given that we get less than two million from the government, most of the money is raised from either donors or our businesses. This means we don't have long-term contracts and thus have to be careful to spend money only when it comes in. While we have done this for each of my past eight years, some years were more difficult than others. A few years ago, we had a particularly difficult year. Donations were down by about 10 percent—either because we didn't employ the right strategies or because it was a midterm election year and a lot of our donors openly said they were going to spend more on elected officials than on nonprofits. Also, during this time, our board was going through a changeover of people, and all of a sudden I needed to spend a huge amount of my time working with the board to ensure our mission stayed on track. I was frustrated and tired, so I wrote to Father Greg.

While writing seems old fashioned and odd given that we see each other often, I found the best exchanges I have with Greg are in the written form. I suppose it forces me to be clearer about my thoughts, and he is able to give the conversation fuller attention than he'd be able to in the commotion of every-day life at the office. Also, he is on the road a great deal, so writing becomes an efficient form of communication.

So, I took time off in January to think quite a bit about the previous year. In my frustration, despair, and feeling of being trapped, I wrote Greg a note:

> Here, it is harder for me to discern what to do. My emotional health over the past year has been unbalanced. All my energies went into "saving the organization" by working to make payroll every two weeks. That was my prism through which I saw nearly all issues (life, friends, co-workers, etc.). Not a good thing, which led me to think, where do I go from here? This week among the books I'm reading, two different ones explain the Jesuit concept of "The Call of the King"—of fortuitous timing. Two quotes have really struck me.
>
>> In the Call of the King, the grace we pray for is not to be deaf to the Lord's call. We should be ready to accomplish the Lord's most holy will. We pray to be open, to be ready, and to be generous. We ask God to give us a generous heart so that we may follow him and be part of the plan. . . . The Call of the King

mobilizes our energy. It invites us to get in touch with our dream of making a better world and to see how Jesus fulfills it.[26]

I have been so thankful for my time at Homeboy. It has led me into a spiritual journey I would have been blind to otherwise. I see and witness God's work here every day. This concept of the Call of the King is action versus just thoughts. It's a commitment to making the work better and is where I still want to be. But what about the strife of the past year? Is it really an example of the concept that sometimes to follow Jesus' path is about hard work and suffering? Clearly, Homeboy is living the dream of making the world better. I understand that I play a role in that, but the scrambling to keep it going, the taking the heat—inside and out—for our failures as an organization, I don't see how this fits with putting my faith into action. That perhaps it's time for me to travel a different path and that's the meaning of the past year? If my path is still at Homeboy, what does it look like? How should I lead differently, how should I bring the team along differently? How do we all get to the point of being in balance and living a generous life?

I'm rested. I've made the decision to not be reactive to my situation but to be proactive. Your thoughts?

A day later, Father Greg responded:

The Call of the King. These things get muddled for us. Often enough we think it's even possible for there to be a gulf between God's will for me AND what I most deeply want. Not true. The great discovery in life is to finally know that what I MOST DEEPLY WANT, IS God's will for me. The trick is "not to be deaf to the Lord's call." IF it ain't a pleasure, it ain't a poem. God's will isn't about "hard work and suffering" but, "My joy yours, your joy complete."

This is the proactive piece (rather than our ingrained reactive piece). Find the joy in the place, this is where I feel I need to be. It's hard, but the call is to joy. Once you flip that switch, you are choosing to see people and to hear people. I'm speaking for myself here. Once

---

26. Gerald M. Fagin, *Putting on the Heart of Christ: How the Spiritual Exercises Invite Us to a Virtuous Life* (Chicago: Loyola Press, 2010), 80.

I decided to choose joy at Homeboy, it became joyful. That is what I most deeply want. God's will. The call of the King.

THEN, people, senior staff, and trainees will feel valued, loved, and received tenderly. Then we can do anything. Otherwise, everyone feels judged, less than, a disappointment. Our default position, cuz we're humans, is to focus on deficits. I do, that's for sure. But when we decide to see unshakable goodness among all the woundedness, people come alive and so do I.

Let's go where the joy is. Let's not settle for happiness, when we're being offered joy. It's here, at Homeboy.

Much, much love

G

So, it's about joy! Father Greg put it so well: "My joy yours, your joy, complete." How do we move to joy in our business life? This is how I thought about it for Homeboy in response to G's letter. I wrote back:

On joy, what you write is very helpful. In fact, I find a lot of joy at Homeboy. I realized that again when I was in for just one day on the third of January. I went home thinking about the joy I experienced. My struggle of late is how to find balance between the joy I experience with you, the trainees, and the team, and all the other aspects of my role that come at me. Many, many folks from the outside—and a good portion of our senior staff—don't have joy in their hearts. They have fear, resentment, "I told you so," and anger. All those emotions come at me, on top of the "Why do you keep running out of money, do something about it" attitudes. I recognize that it is my role to handle these situations and to shield the organization from the worst of it. I'm not whining; I'm just trying to find another way. People are their best selves in front of you—as they should—but sometimes overcompensate the other way when dealing with me. We need to find a way to bring everybody to joy, to the joy of Homeboy.

I've been thinking a lot about our senior team and the current culture we have right now. I think it's devoid of joy, devoid of people working on themselves, devoid of finding goodness in each other. Right now it's just a mix of liking what they do, liking the idea of being part of Homeboy, holding on tight to their part of the whole, feeling like a victim in some cases (this situation is mostly from the outside staff, not those who have grown up in the program). Up until now, we have let the organizational culture evolve organically. I think that has left us with what we got—a mixed bag. If we can get a majority of the team to go to joy, then we will be in great shape. How do we do that? How do we move the organization to joy when joy is being offered? You and I need to figure this one out, and it is an example of how both of our roles need to evolve to make the organization healthier.

That is what we decided to do: work to move the organization to joy. That work I knew would start with me. I can't ask others to look for the joy in their lives and in our community without doing the same. I personally became reengaged. I worked to find my joy, to find my joy in kinship with others. Archbishop Desmond Tutu said, "We have at home the concept of Ubuntu—a person is a person through other persons." I proactively thought about how to find joy through others. There are no step-by-step instructions; it's a mindset, a belief that being in relationship with others brings joy, particularly when you look for it.

In their *Book of Joy*, Archbishop Desmond Tutu and His Holiness Dalai Lama write, "Joy is much bigger than happiness. While happiness is often seen as dependent on external circumstances, joy is not."[27] Father Greg speaks of finding joy in terms of not when, but *where*. My joy begins when I feel in union with God. I also find joy in kinship with our homies. I find joy when I'm present to observe our trainees revel in being parents. When they share with me about going to their child's school Halloween parade, or the joy they felt watching their son get a haircut. It's found in the moments of kinship. Of joyfully playing with their kids. When the homies come into the office and proudly share about their time in kinship with their families, it fills my heart with warmth and brings joy to my soul. If I were not present with a humble, patient, and gentle mindset as God teaches us, the joy that is available through kinship in these moments with our folks would be fleeting for me.

One of my favorite days at Homeboy is our annual family picnic. We pick a Friday in early summer, right after school is let out, and invite all our trainees

---

27. His Holiness Dalai Lama and Archbishop Desmond Tutu, *The Book of Joy* (New York: Penguin Random House, 2016), 196.

and staff to bring their families and celebrate. We reserve a spot at Elysian Park, a large, old park in Los Angeles, which sits in the shadows of Dodger Stadium. The space we reserve is quite large and has enough room for a baseball or kickball game to occur at the same time as a flag football game. There is enough space for each family to lay out a blanket and put out a few chairs.

Over the years we learned not to have this picnic on a payday—we pay every other week—because many folks are anxious as payday approaches. When bank accounts are low, the energy is understandably not as easygoing. So, on the scheduled day, we begin at our main building with our traditional morning meeting, and then we all carpool over to the park, which is less than two miles away. Some of our senior leaders arrive at the park hours in advance to set up the tables, chairs, game areas, and most important, to start cooking on the grills. When people show up at nine thirty, they are ready to eat like it's lunchtime. One of my favorite activities is our kickball tournament. We started with softball but discovered that more people play if we make it kickball. The teams are a mix of senior staff and the trainees they are tight with, kids with adults, men and women, boys and girls. While there is a competitive spirit, it's all in good fun, for the adults really want their children to have a good time and participate. The sense of pride our trainees have in the organization is visible. They go out of their way to introduce their children to everybody. They share their blankets with each other, and while they are shy about participating in some of the sporting events, they really enjoy being around one another. I find it reenergizing to see our trainees in a more relaxed situation, enjoying themselves and seeking community with others, with their families around. It's not often that their families get to see this side of them. Our family picnic celebration is a day filled with warmth, smiles all around, sharing of food, and finding joy through being in kinship with one another.

I asked my spiritual advisor about joy. He said that joy is the infallible sign of the presence of God. I now know that without a doubt, Homeboy is joy and I just need to open my heart and let it in. All of us who work in an organization experience some form of this problem of how to get to joy. Our goal as leaders is to facilitate organizational joy as we, on an individual level, move ourselves to joy. A joy that is pure, that is openhearted, and that is humble.

In pondering joy, I was able to go from feeling "put upon" by my responsibilities to feeling that my responsibilities are part of my life's mission. I learned that the key is about discovering and experiencing joy. Who doesn't want to achieve this next level of awareness? It's real and it's in front of me—I just need to open my eyes and heart to see it, as the homies do.

Interesting, that after so many years of hard work and worry, when I understood this concept of joy, it was a quick shift for me. Like a switch being flipped in my brain. Now all the hard work and worries seem small and inconsequential compared to the quest for and attaining of joy.

Joy is foundational in a thriving workplace.

CHAPTER 9

SPIRITUAL JOURNEY

So how do I blend what I know works in capitalism with my experiences at Homeboy, to what I want to change about capitalism? How do we create a bridge between the Two Americas? Are being a corporate executive and spiritually joyful mutually exclusive? Eventually I discovered that there's a fourth leg of the conceptual stool that I was missing. It was to understand God better. I recognized that my own spirituality was a bit shallow. I had to find an understanding that was more substantive and gave me better grounding. I had to mature a lot more in my spiritual growth, in my understanding of God and how to live—and lead—in a faith-based way that is inclusive of all.

I had lived a good life—even a charmed life—by the adage of "to whom much is given, much must be returned." I grew up in a pretty straightforward Italian-American family. Although we were Sunday churchgoers, we did not do much Bible reading. Our parents taught us morals and that we should try to help others. We grew up with no pretense, no expectations that the world would give us anything but that we must earn our way. We didn't grow up thinking much about our own spirituality. I modeled my parenting after my parents. I taught my children to live a good, clean life, to worship God, and to respect others. I happily lived in this mode until I joined Homeboy. I didn't know any other way to be. I joined Homeboy to give back, expecting nothing in return. In fact, I not only did not expect anything in return, I also didn't want anything in return. But I did get something in return: a priceless invitation to pursue my own spiritual growth.

One day, a year into my time there, one of our senior leaders, Mary Ellen Burton, asked, "Have you figured out why you are here?" I said, "Sure, it's because I can do X and implement Y and that I was asked by a board member to get involved to do just that." She patiently waited for me to finish, then said, "I think you are here because God has intended it to be that way." I first thought that was such a nice thing to say, but honestly, in that moment, I didn't believe it.

Being around Homeboy, you can't avoid having its spirituality-soaked approach to people affect your view on life. Particularly with Father Greg's focus on shining a light on the goodness of all people. Writer G. K. Chesterton said, "A saint is one who exaggerates what the world neglects." There is no doubt in my mind that Father Greg is a saint, always exaggerating the notion that "no one is disposable." It has become a Homeboy motto.

It's been very special for me to be in Greg's orbit, for I have been able to absorb and discover a great deal. That being said, some of the best lessons I've learned are from being with the trainees, the homies, when I get to observe how they talk authentically about their trauma and struggle with life and yet how their words of wisdom are as pure as any spoken word from a great authority. How, in the face of extreme poverty and a brutal life of trauma, they find pure joy in each other, in family, in their relationship with God. They experience God in a way that many of us can't. In the Beatitudes, Matthew 5:3, when Jesus says, "Blessed are the poor in spirit; theirs is the kingdom of Heaven," he is talking about our folks who have found the joy of God. They are the ones with no pretense, no need for status, no need to see themselves over others; they are humble. These folks are a step closer to God, for they have a clearer faith and more enduring hope.

I recall one long journey by car when my friend Dave and I were traveling with two of our homegrown leaders, José and Robert, back from completing a hike up Mt. Whitney. Dave began riffing on the story of the Prodigal Son.

This story of redemption appears in Luke 15:11–32 and describes two brothers who are set to inherit their father's fortune. The younger brother asks for it and is given it—but wastes it. Upon failing, that son, filled with shame, asks his father to allow him to return as his servant so as to redeem himself.

His father welcomes him home with open arms, celebrating his return with festivities. The older son refuses to participate in the festivities, envious of his father's love for his brother. To this his father says, "Son, you are always with me, and all that is mine is yours. But we had to celebrate and rejoice, because this brother of yours was dead and has come to life; he was lost and has been found" (Luke 15:32).

As José and Robert began "chopping it up," Dave and I went quiet and just listened to them. We were in awe of how deeply the two understood the parable, how they related it to their lives and their relationship with God. In those moments, I realized how much I can learn from José's and Robert's relationships with God. I greatly admired their depth of understanding, their trust in the meaning, and their shared knowledge of what they had learned. I began to question why I didn't have this same depth, trust, and understanding of God's word inside me. From then on, I tried to pay more attention to my relationship with God and to my spiritual journey. What lessons do I take from these parables; how can I elevate them from a superficial level and really reflect upon my life and move my spiritual path forward? I treasure those moments in the car with Robert and José, when they showed me the magnificence of having a deeper relationship with God.

Learning to "Sweat"

One of our ambitions in the organization is to show the world what we do and why we do it—because there's goodness in everybody. One way we do this is by giving a lot of tours of our Los Angeles headquarters. Organizations visit us, learn what we do, then take back our materials and our model to their local community to create similar organizations. In fact, each year more than ten thousand people tour Homeboy Industries and experience what we know to be true: community trumps gangs. Some of these tour groups are religious organizations. Their most frequent questions include, "Are you a religious organization; do you have Bible study, and do you teach the gospel?" In fact, we're not a religious organization, and we do not teach the gospel. However, as Father Greg would say, "we're soaked in spirituality." It is that spirituality that really is the backbone of what makes the organization successful. People here find their own spirituality, they find their own path, they find goodness, they experience joy and allow it to grow. That's what helps transform their lives.

People here pray to their perception of God, in their own way, in their own style. There is no singular approach. There's a strong presence of Native American spirituality and beliefs at Homeboy, which has been integrated into our culture by many clients and trainees over the years. Our folks really enjoy hearing Native American folklore and learning how Native Americans approach the god or the gods they pray to. In fact, throughout the year many members of our community participate in a "sweat," a Native American spirituality practice. I was invited to go to one of these retreats at a sweat lodge. It was located not out in the wilderness but in the backyard of a house in East Los Angeles. With some hesitation—yet a desire to learn—I accepted.

The week before going to this sweat—me being me and trying to understand what was going on—I started asking questions. "What do I need to do, how do I prepare, how does it go?" Hector gave me advice and hints for getting through it. He said, "It's hard, because when you go into this teepee, after the hot rocks go in, the heat and steam build up, and it gets very hot and very intense." He explained that as you sit on the ground inside the teepee, the prayers and chants come forward along with the heat, and as you pray, it gets far more intense. Hector suggested that once I was in the tent, to get as low as possible, and when I thought I couldn't take it any longer, put my face right on the dirt—as that would be the coolest part of the teepee—so I would be able to breathe better and hang in there.

The fear rose as I considered all this: would I be able to last the whole session? When the time came, we piled into the van and drove to the sweat lodge. There were about fifteen of us, so we took turns. There were two facilitators there: one was to be in the tent with us to chant, pray, and lead, and the other manned the fire, bringing hot stones into the teepee. Wearing few clothes, we went in and sat on the ground. The stones were brought in, and slowly, the chants began. I felt suddenly transported and transformed into this experience that has been in practice for thousands of years. The folks who were experienced with these sweats quickly got in the mode of praying, of thanking God. For those who felt the experience move them, perhaps because they were going through pain, chanting and praying provided a way to release the pain. There were wails, there were screams, there were tears—but also a sense of community. In that tent, no one was alone.

I didn't want to embarrass myself, and I didn't want to disrespect what was going on. So when it got to my time to say something, I passed the first time and waited for the second time, opting to continue observing for a while longer. When the second time came around, the tent was even hotter, and I didn't know if I was more light-headed or less hydrated. I just began feeling very uncomfortable. Then something in me moved to reflect on the pain in my life and to use this opportunity as a way of purging that pain. As I surrendered to my pain with the group, a sense of peace flooded in. I no longer felt so uncomfortable and greatly enjoyed the rhythmic chanting thereafter.

About halfway through, the flaps were opened and a gust of fresh cool air came through the space. I was revived for a little bit. Before the vent was closed, more rocks were brought in. As the heat came up, the sweat began pouring off me, and I got back to meditating and thinking again. With chanting going on in the background, I thought of Hector and thanked him for the advice to stay low and get in the dirt; I was grateful for the moisture I found there. I felt more alive than ever before. When the sweat ended, we came out of the tent and washed ourselves off. We shared some food and exchanged notes, then embarked on our way home. I think about that sweat lodge quite a bit. I'd never experienced anything like it. I was touched at how the others had welcomed me into their world, though a bit mysterious, nothing hidden from me. They were eager to teach, eager to explain, and proud of the traditions. In many ways, this experience embodies what Homeboy is about. We come into what we call a cathedral at Homeboy Industries, a sanctuary, where we share and talk through our pain, live our life in community and in peace with one another—then move on.

These experiences help me see God in a different way, through different eyes and different cultures. They help me see how important it is to be open to new experiences and perspectives. How can I, the $6MDM, really get on this path? Have I been too trained, too corrupted by the material world? How am I to figure this out? Am I too old for it to have any practical significance?

Can the $6MDM really open his heart? Had my heart been outfitted with too much armor so that I could succeed in the corporate world?

Spiritual teacher and writer Richard Rohr says, "The higher and more visible you are in any system, the more trapped you are inside it. The freest position is the one I call 'on the edge of the inside,' neither a company man nor a rebel or iconoclast. The price of both holding power and speaking truth to power can be very great. You ricochet between being offensive and being defensive, neither of which is a contemplative or a solid position. Further, you are forced to either defend and maintain the status quo to protect yourself and the group or to waste time reacting against it. My fellow teacher Cynthia Bourgeault calls this 'pouring empty into empty.'"[28] It's a path nowhere close to a spiritual awakening.

How many of us these days spend our time justifying our positions, our status, our tribe, our nationalism, and so on? It's pouring empty into empty. How many of us put effort into defending our titles or pushing for the next title, competing for the next rung on the ladder, all for sheer egoism, displaying power in the office over staff, pitting one work group against another? All of this is pouring empty into empty. For most of my adult life I was doing exactly this.

Understanding this and seeing that I was not nearly as spiritually aware as the people of Homeboy, made me hungry to know more, to experience more, and to understand more. I finally decided that, "Yes, I'm on a journey. So be smarter, be more open about it, go experience new things."

Transcendental Meditation

Many of our Homeboy trainees are victims of complex trauma—often from the time they were young children. It's not uncommon for patterns of abuse to get repeated in the next generation. Quite a bit of our time and energy are focused on helping our folks heal and end this cycle of violence. This includes various types of group therapies and group encounters. Although most of our folks are functional in everyday life, those memories and traumatic experiences are never too far away.

---

28. Richard Rohr, "Blessed Are the Poor in Spirit," adapted from Richard Rohr, *Jesus' Plan for a New World* (Cincinnati, OH: Franciscan Media, 1996), 129, 130–31, https://cac.org.

It's no surprise that things can get real—awfully fast. For example, there may be a men's, women's, or mixed therapy session of folks who are abusers or a group of folks who are victims of violence. A key aspect of having these groups together is how they are run, how they are modeled, and how they are facilitated. As a senior staff team, we try a lot of these experiences ourselves. We've gone through healing circles; we've used the ritual burning of sage; we have retreats and many different types of group therapies together. We're open to new experiences and new ways of healing together. One of them is transcendental meditation.

Several years ago, actor and comedian Jim Carrey asked to visit Homeboy. He met with Father Greg and had lunch in the Homegirl Café with a couple of the homies. Jim was terrific. He was friendly, always smiling, and engaging with our trainees. Over the years, many famous people have come through Homeboy, but for some reason, Jim seemed to be the star among stars. People were jazzed to see him: they had seen his movies, and they could cite his lines—and he was good-natured about it. When someone would quote him from one of his early movies, he would quote back and ham it up with them. At one point, Jim asked to come back to visit Homeboy again to see if he could help. He was welcomed back with open arms and led one of our morning meetings. His message was emotional and heartfelt.[29] Jim felt called to facilitate transcendental meditation courses for us because he sees transcendental meditation as a way of finding one's inner peace and balance. A way for anyone who has that ongoing meter and ticker in their head—compelling them to move faster—to get calm, meditate, and think things through.

Through Jim's Better U Foundation, several transcendental meditation instructors came in and taught more than fifty of us how to do this practice. They began with our trainees, some of whom also went through a "Teach the Teachers" program and learned to run their own transcendental meditation groups. Many of our trainees found this quite valuable and learned that spending twenty minutes each day meditating allowed them to slow their busy minds and find more space to work through the pain of their trauma. Over

---

29. Jim Carrey, "This Room Is Filled with God," Homeboy Industries YouTube video, September 9, 2017, https://www.youtube.com/watch?v=MzyaQ0H5D74.

time, they found that they were happier and more positive. After the first couple of groups went through the transcendental meditation program, it was opened to everyone. So, every morning at nine fifteen, those in our organization who felt inclined would go off and do transcendental meditation for thirty minutes. People asked me if I would try it or if I'd attended the session and learned how to do it. I said I would.

The crucial step in transcendental meditation is not simply learning it but practicing it consistently. My transcendental meditation instructor told me that the best thing to do is to commit oneself to it for at least forty-five days, practicing twenty minutes in the morning and at least ten to fifteen minutes late in the day. As a good, overachieving student and type A personality, once I committed to it, I was determined to see it through. In my first session, my transcendental meditation instructor guided me with instructions, then took me through the quietness of the practice with a mantra I was to repeat quietly in my mind. The point was to stop thinking, to center on myself, and to work to keep outside thoughts from entering my mind. Even in that first session, as short as it was, I discovered that I could in fact quiet my brain and settle down, though I found it hard to empty my brain and to stop thinking of things. With practice, I learned to shut down disruptive thoughts quickly and return to my mantra.

For the next forty-five days, I practiced transcendental meditation every day. I found, without a doubt, that it helped me stay calmer and more positive overall. While it was hard at first to schedule the time to practice, I shifted my routine and began getting up a bit earlier each morning to get my practice in before the day started. I found that I was fresher as I began my day and was able to remain calmer in the face of the day's events. I found great value in transcendental meditation, just as many of our trainees did. However, toward the end of my forty-five-day practice commitment, I felt that I was missing something. Transcendental meditation did not seem to connect that much to my Christian spirituality, so I phased out of that and sought other types of meditation and contemplation. Now my meditation focuses on my relationship with God. I probably would not have come to this, however, without the help of the transcendental meditation, which taught me to calm myself and my thoughts. I was able to apply those skills to the development of my faith.

Seeking Spiritual Clarity

Over the first few years, I directed my spiritual questions to Father Greg, who never failed to respond with insight, clarity, and a consistent philosophy of an ever-loving God. These exchanges encouraged my faith and helped deepen my friendship with Father Greg. Then I began reading books on spirituality. In the world of spirituality books, there are a lot of different flavors, and finding a style that resonated with me was not easy. I asked for book recommendations and found a lot of great books out there. I love reading books, especially while I'm on vacation. I can spend the whole day on the beach under an umbrella reading. I realized that the best time of day to read about Jesus, the saints, and spiritual growth is in the late afternoon as the sun fades in the west. During this time, I pick my head up, look at the sky, and meditate on what I have just read. Often, it feels like "the heavens" or God is talking to me, filling me up, glowing around me—this is my piece of heaven.

There are several folks at Homeboy who regularly seek spiritual direction from an advisor. I asked Father Greg about this, and he wholeheartedly endorsed the idea and set me up with a spiritual advisor. After Greg introduced me to Gordon, I hesitated and waited a few more months before going to my first session. I was nervous and afraid that my lack of biblical knowledge would show through. How would it look for the CEO of Homeboy to be such a dunce in the realm of spirituality and biblical teachings? (I know now these are separate notions, but back then I felt somewhat ignorant about both.)

When I finally arrived for my first session with Gordon, he sensed my nervousness and was wonderful about putting me at ease. In fact, we spent much of the first session just talking about people we knew in common—Greg for sure—and near the end of the session, we talked about what spiritual direction was, and he asked me to think seriously about whether I wanted to go forward. He said, "Your life will change, and you will need to just trust the process." I paused. My life would change? I already had a great life—my wonderful wife and family. Why would I want to change all that? I had a real fear that I might discover something about myself that would move me emotionally further away from my family. At the end of the first session, I made an appointment to meet again, but I knew I had some thinking to do. I went home and talked to my wife. While neither one of us really knew in depth what was meant by "spiritual direction," she gave me her full support and the confidence to move forward.

The next several months were eye-opening. I prepared for the sessions by reading articles, books, and listing all my questions. I eagerly waited to get to the next session so I could get my questions answered. While I approached each session this way, that's not the way it played out. Gordon might provide a kind-of answer, but then he would push it back on me to dig deeper into my own thoughts as to what something meant. This style of interaction gave me the confidence to see something for myself and make my own conclusions—independent of any orthodoxy. I had somewhat assumed that there was a single best answer when it came to Christian teachings, and I didn't know those answers because I had never studied the Bible. Here the philosophy is to take the simple, authentic concepts of Christianity and use them as a frame for all questions that arise. The Jesuits have a notion that if a word or a phrase doesn't work for you—in terms of leading to deeper understanding—forget about it and move on. This is another lesson that was freeing for me. I was one of those types who would stubbornly stay on an issue or a phrase until I could understand it and thought it was a failing of mine to give up on something I couldn't comprehend.

Today, these are my simply stated and basic learnings: God is too busy loving us to judge us. We shouldn't judge others. Sin is about not engaging with God. Hell is when we have darkness, don't acknowledge God, or find ourselves in a place without God forever. Heaven is here with us now. God doesn't "allow" suffering; God is always around us and our goal is to feel God's love even through suffering. Jesus' suffering did not diminish His love for us. There is goodness in everybody. There isn't a moment when God is not trying to communicate with us. Mercy is a gift and is also a duty. Jesus showed us we can move through suffering because of His grace and love. Openness to grace allows grace to happen. God loves what God has created.

My Examen

In my spiritual direction, which was grounded in Jesuit teachings, I was encouraged to do the daily *examen*, a form of prayer and meditation. I anticipated that it was going to be challenging because I'd never been a daily-prayer type of guy. I would often ponder God when I was at church and would formally "pray," but I didn't make a practice of even a bedtime prayer. I saw this as another personal spiritual failing, as if I had been missing out on an opportunity to connect with God more intimately. So, in my typical mode, I went off and read a book—or two—about the *examen*, which in retrospect is a bit silly, since it's an easy prayer practice to learn.

I found *a simple, life-changing prayer* by Jim Manney to be a particularly useful guide for this practice. The daily *examen* is about being contemplative through five straightforward steps. Here is how I have interpreted the steps, and I humbly ask for apologies from the experts for any misarticulation of this five-hundred-year-old tradition.

Pray for light: Acknowledge God and ask for strength and humility to accept his help. Notice that God is with me and see that God is seeing me.

Give thanks: Thanks and gratitude for being loved by God, being one who is received by God, and recognizing that everything is a gift of God.

Review the day (prior day) hour by hour: When was I closest to God? When was I furthest? How did that feel? Can I see God in all of it?

Look at what's wrong: Face up to my failures and shortcomings. Were there times when I didn't encounter others in the way I feel reflects my values? Sit with those notions and ask God to show me the way to improve.

Resolve the day to come: Where does God need me to be today? How do I stay humble? What do I want God to teach me today? How would God have me act wisely?

The *examen* is not a self-reflection but a form of communing with God. *Examen* is a method of finding God in one's life as it is being lived right now. It's a daily reflection on life with God. This is something I would have never thought to do, yet it is now a vital part of my day and keeps me energized, focused, emotionally balanced, and connected to God.

Enough Suffering?

I often feel that I haven't suffered enough or that my suffering is so minor compared to the suffering of the people we help at Homeboy. Can I ever be as "holy" as those who have suffered and transformed their lives? Can I ever achieve the spiritual growth I am seeking and become closer to God without ever having to depend on God to see me through difficult times? I would not say I've ever experienced a "dark" time in my life, but those experiences that seem dark to me don't even compare to the dark times others have experienced. Doubts creep in and I wonder, *Will I ever make it through my spiritual journey if I lived too good of a life?*

In the famous work *Dark Night of the Soul*, John of the Cross (1542–1591) says, "The Divine disentangles and dissolves her spiritual substance, absorbing it in deep darkness. In the face of her own misery, the soul feels herself coming undone and melting away in a cruel, spiritual death."[30] The thinking here is that it is in this darkness where spiritual death of the old self leads to a new self, born with God. But for me, I think, *Wait. I've not had this most serious suffering whereby I've found myself in this darkness, experiencing a spiritual death.*

I haven't done a long prison term. I haven't spent time in the SHU (Security Housing Unit). I haven't done crimes and therefore, I'm not haunted by the guilt. I have never been homeless. I was not abused by my parents. I was never addicted to narcotics. I never had to deal with loneliness; my wife didn't leave me. I never went hungry. I'm not a victim of domestic violence. I did not serve in a war. I had "normal" suffering, such as my parents' passing away, workplace disappointments, parental stress, feelings of being out of control—life just not being easy. My experiences pale in comparison to real deep sufferings I witness every day at Homeboy. So without that sort of deep suffering, will I ever find God?

I asked my friend Mary Ellen her perspective on what is meant by "the soul feels herself coming undone." She said, "My sense is that 'feels' is an important word in your sentence." She explained that when the divine lays siege to our souls, it can feel as if we are being destroyed. All our constructs, ideas, identity, and beliefs are stripped away. It's a little like living in a well-constructed shell that the divine breaks open—which brings us out into a new life. It feels like death. Maybe it's because we thought that the life we had in the shell was

---

30. John of the Cross, *Dark Night of the Soul*, trans. Mirabai Starr (New York: Penguin Putnam, Inc., 2002), chapter 6.

all there ever could be. We thought we had it all figured out and had things under control, so we would be protected from pain and suffering. Our imaginations were too small, and the joy, deep connection, and freedom that the "stripping" brings are beyond us. It's so, so hard to let go of the "habitual affections and attachments to the old self." When suffering rips it away, it's even more painful. It feels as if something was done to us to harm us.

Jesuit philosophy encourages us to move on from a concept if it doesn't work for us. So, I then asked, could the divine lay siege to our souls without it feeling like we are being destroyed? It seems obvious to say yes, right? Is there a need to suffer to "get it," or is this written for folks who have suffered greatly and thus need to put their suffering in some type of order? A central theme I keep coming back to is this notion of suffering. Is suffering God's plan for us to get to know him better?

Unfortunately, my spiritual advisor, Gordon, retired due to illness. I'm thankful for him and to Father Greg for recommending a new spiritual advisor, Randy, with whom I can continue. So I turned to Randy with these questions about suffering. He suggested that it's not God's plan to have us suffer. The better question to ask is how God has been with me in crisis as opposed to focusing on whether I suffered enough to be closer to Him. Instead, use the gifts that God has given me, knowing that He is always loving and yet we hurt. God knows pain. He knows what it feels like from the inside, and He is in it compassionately with us.

Pay attention to the gifts we have. We each have different gifts, so use what we have in prayer and meditation on what God would want us to do with those gifts. There is not you and a spiritual you; there is just you. The spiritual path does not rely on great suffering; rather, it's finding your gifts and deciding what God wants you to do with them.

Seeing God

During the third step of the *examen*, I ask the Holy Spirit to guide me through a review of the day just completed. As I do this each morning, I find that when I do the *examen* in the morning, I'm much more aware, alert, and insightful than I am at the end of a long day. In this step, the task is to see God's presence around me and my responses to it. The answer is easy for the week-days, the time I spend at Homeboy. I've said to many visitors of Homeboy that the most apparent place to see God's presence in our lives is within the community there. It's so apparent, it practically smacks you in the face—from our morning meeting with a thought of the day given by a trainee or staff member to conversations with the community about their healing, to the extension of uninhibited kinship.

My difficulty comes on Sunday and Monday mornings, when I look back on the previous day where it's my very ordinary life. How do I see God's presence there? With my well-to-do friends? During a healthy but routine home-life? After months of doing the daily *examen*, I finally shared with my advisor that it just doesn't seem to work when I'm home. I may have been the first person ever to phrase it that way to him. He then asked me a series of questions, including, "Why do you think that?" Gordon continued, "Why wouldn't God be with you at home? Why do you think God is only with you at Homeboy?" The point is that I'm to figure this one out, since it's clear God is always with me. It's on me to pray on why I can't see Him very well at home.

I think the answer is that it has to do with me. At Homeboy I can observe and be present to witness God's presence, but really, it should be about me participating and reflecting on God's presence within me. What have I done? How have I thought of a situation? What is my role in God's presence?

Both my concerns about suffering and seeing God have to do with me and how I view my relationship with God. How well do I take a step back and allow my eyes to be open to Him, to allow my brain to be attuned to absorbing His message, and how open is my heart to grace?

Why share about my spiritual journey? Is it for everyone? The point for me is that without the benefit of what I've learned so far on my journey, my life would be out of balance. I would constantly be stressed about work struggles, and I would make these "problems" front and center all the time. These struggles would define who I am and how I view others. A life defined by a work-place would be not only frustrating but dark.

Here I am today, having traveled so very far along my spiritual path compared with where I started, but not very far in the bigger picture. I have so much more to learn, to experience, to understand, to digest. I now understand that this journey has no destination. It's about continually going deeper and being more open to God being in my life every day, using my God-given gifts to help others, and doing my work with grace and love.

Finding Joy

I am so grateful for my e-mail exchanges with Father Greg on bringing the organization to joy. I was exasperated, wanted to stop, and no longer felt that the work was fulfilling. I realized I was pouring empty into empty. So I made a conscious decision to fill myself with something greater than myself. I couldn't give, let alone model, what I didn't have. I am grateful that I embarked on a journey of spiritual development. I'm grateful that I've come to understand and experience joy. I'm grateful to those in the Homeboy community who so wisely saw why I was here long before I had any clue, and for their patience with me along the way. In the last couple of years, there hasn't been one moment where I thought I'd had enough. I'm now locked in and know what I want to do. What God wants me to do.

I wonder if there's something in my story that helps whoever reads this book get to a point where they're locked in. A place where they know where they are, why they do what they do, and are able to see the bigger picture.

Homeboy is the place where I started my spiritual journey to learn more about God and myself. I was to give Homeboy all I had, and in return, I gained far more. Through humbling myself to learn from those around me, I can experience God so much more. My continuing questions are, How do I blend my spiritual path with the evolution of Homeboy? What is the future going to be for Homeboy—and for me?

CHAPTER 10

LEADERSHIP DEVELOPMENT FOR RACIAL EQUITY

A few years back, Father Greg and I had a series of dialogues around the future of Homeboy. He had been doing this work for thirty years, and I had been there the last five. Whether independently or by influencing each other, we realized that keeping the operation afloat wasn't getting any easier. In fact, we were in a twenty-month stretch that seemed increasingly more difficult. The root issue was that we weren't raising enough money in a consistent fashion. While we are blessed with generous donors, they are unpredictable, and it's not prudent to be so dependent on their gifts. In that fiscal year, contributions accounted for ten million dollars, a number that most other human-service nonprofits would envy. However, in that year we had expected eleven million from donors, which led to a million-dollar shortfall at the end of the fiscal year. Thus, we scrambled the following year to stretch every dollar, working hard to raise money for the current year and to make up for the previous year's shortfall.

When I say we worked hard, it was almost like begging, which has a downside, for when donors sense desperation, it becomes harder to raise the funds. People naturally want to invest in a winner. Some of our staff are turned off by the begging, but I have no problem with it, for I know I do it to help the homies. I know that without this money, many more people will be turned away from our program—and the cost of failure is huge. Father Greg has always been a great partner when asking for money; however, I sensed a fatigue in him as well. How many times do we have to keep groveling before we can get to a point where we are well funded and secure?

Nearly all the other human-service organizations are funded through government resources. For Homeboy, that accounts for less than 5 percent of our total revenues. While other organizations need to worry about renewing their long-term contracts for their sustainability, they, unlike Homeboy, avoid the payroll-to-payroll scramble for funds. Yet significant government funds still elude us.

What Will We Need for the Long Term?

As I sat back and surveyed the field, I found it mind-boggling that we have Father Greg—who is as close to a living saint as there is—and still must worry every year about getting the support we need. Father Greg is also a fundraising megastar. Through his spoken words and actions, a movement has been created, and people generously donate. But those funds are barely enough to serve all the people who come through our doors. Here I am, with a self-proclaimed $6MDM skill set, co-leading an organization, and I can't seem to get us over the hump in terms of long-term sustainability. I sometimes thought that perhaps they needed a different leader to reach this goal. I don't take a salary, and Father Greg doesn't get paid much either. If Homeboy can't afford us, how can the organization afford someone else?

In the corporate world, succession planning is of utmost concern for top management. The focus of the concern is obvious: if something happened to the top leadership (i.e., "hit by a bus"), how would the organization survive, let alone thrive? For corporations it's about who will be in charge to make sure the business model continues to function and profits still churn out so that people retain their jobs and shareholders continue to be rewarded. My observations were that for Homeboy, clearly if something happened to Father Greg, our organization would be in deep trouble from a money standpoint. Less so, but still true, is that if I were to leave, the organization would struggle along, then go into a decline. I felt that my skill set was the glue holding the businesses together.

In business speak, we were at an inflection point. Knowing we were getting older and I, at least, was getting run-down, the question was, should we just unwind the organization and have a slow shutdown while both of us are still here? Philosophically, it's not a bad outcome. For the past several years, we have helped thousands and thousands of people. Through the open doors of Homeboy, so many people were able to improve their lives, transform their pain, be loved for the first time, and achieve economic stability. If Homeboy ceased to exist, it would be a shame and disappointing, but it wouldn't take away from all the good work that has occurred. The measurement of a mission is not whether it continues for another hundred years but whether it helps people. If the community support (donors, elected officials, business patrons) isn't there while everything is being run as best it can be, then perhaps that effort wasn't made to last—maybe it was just for a chapter in time.

However, the business side of me, the learned instinct to always win, was fighting the urge to close. There must be a better way for the organization to achieve long-term prosperity and have a strong team of leaders take it into the future.

In my view, we needed two things to get on track for long-term sustainability: (1) an endowment and (2) further development of the leadership team. Could we possibly raise significantly more funds in a year to provide a reserve and an endowment? We were barely covering our operating expenses. Could we have a donor put five million dollars into a long-term reserve that would provide the necessary security so we could think and act from a longer-term perspective? Could the senior leadership team, filled with former clients, step up enough to run the day-to-day operations? Would the board be comfortable with internal leaders taking on more responsibility and not look to the outside for replacements? I pondered all these questions often. When I'm on a panel discussion at a conference and someone asks me, "What keeps you up at night?" without a doubt it's whether Homeboy can make it in the future without Father Greg and me.

Before I threw in the towel, I decided to take one more crack at it. I was more hopeful about finding the money than I was about developing the management team. The struggles with the management team were threefold. First, would they be willing to learn new skills to become top-tier senior leaders? Second, would they be able to achieve the necessary collective attitude when they were mostly in the mode of worrying about themselves (or the clients)—but not about one another? We needed to change the senior team morale, to give everyone a fair chance, but if they couldn't positively contribute, they should leave, no matter how good they are with the clients. Finally, I knew I needed to groom more former trainees into the management ranks.

It was in the best interest of the organization's sustainability plan to remove the negative people from management. It's what all good organizations do. You can't have someone who consistently brings down the group with their own issues. However, at Homeboy, we are allergic to this type of thinking because we are a place of compassion and second chances. These ideas often get muddled and organization paralysis sets in. For me to take one more shot at getting the organization stable for the future, we needed some people to move on. When they did, it was painful, but the management team became much healthier as a result.

On the morale front, we conducted a series of off-site meetings to learn more about one another and really make the effort to move the team to joy. A key component was a spiritual retreat with the management team. The goal was to better understand the spiritual underpinnings of the organization and to individually seek our own comfort level with Homeboy's approach. As the corporate guy, I went into this off-site very hesitantly because, for all my career up until my work at Homeboy, I had learned not to mix business and spirituality. The meeting turned out to be good, safe, and affirming. I believe this meeting, and subsequent gatherings, helped raise the organization morale through participants learning to extend to one another more generosity and gratitude. Additionally, our board chair conducted a series of womens leadership retreats, which has played a vital role in developing our senior management focus to this end.

Challenges to Leadership Development

The struggle for any organization is to develop the next generation of leaders, and at Homeboy it's not only vitally important to the mission but also an order of magnitude more difficult. Our population needs to see people like themselves in leadership roles so that actions we take are authentic and have the best interest of the client in mind. In the early years, Father Greg *was* the leadership. His street cred allowed him to lead in true authenticity the community we serve. As the organization grows and time passes, the leadership team will need to have former trainees leading the implementation of the mission.

The typical company has the luxury of hiring into their organization mid- to high-level managers and can groom them to become the top leadership. For Homeboy, to have leaders who share the lived experiences and histories of those we serve—gang life, incarceration, and trauma—we need to groom our people from the very bottom, up. They start as clients, and when they are ready, become frontline core workers, which is followed by a series of supervisory jobs before they get into middle management. Once in middle management, they have attained a combination of positive leadership and a few functional skills. However, moving beyond middle management at Homeboy or at any organization becomes a question of how many other functional skills one can attain along the way. When someone becomes a senior leader, they function as a general manager. This is where the task becomes the largest challenge, for it's in part about motivation of the individual and the ability of the organization to provide such learning experiences.

As for motivation, it's complicated for our clients. One of Father Greg's insights is that young people who are stuck in the gang lifestyle don't see themselves living past thirty years of age. (This is one reason why tougher sentencing laws don't deter crime: these young people don't believe their life is going to last long anyway.) So when they come to Homeboy, it's the first time they have started dreaming and planning for a long life. Once they make it through our eighteen-month program, they rightly feel as if they have accomplished something magical. "What's next, and how do I move up the corporate ladder?" is still far away from their thinking. Many just want to revel in the life they now have, "the good life." I've had many conversations with trainees who make that first leap to management, and they are thrilled and don't even want to think about the next step. They are now a success to their children, their families, their friends, and themselves.

Another aspect of developing a career is that you need self-awareness about your "work flaws." When our homies reach "the good life," it is after so much deep introspection to transform their lives that they avoid considering yet another level of introspection regarding work life. This period of calm can last a few years. Then, for some, they begin to want more and develop further. When this time arrives, we can begin discussions about further development of business and managerial skills.

We have to keep in mind that the only organizational structure our homies have known is gang hierarchy, which is wholly different from structures in the nonprofit, grassroots-based world and the corporate world of matrix organizations. In the gang world, the leader gets to make a call, and everyone needs to follow and listen. Thus, when our people from within become managers at Homeboy for the first time, they expect absolute authority, which rarely ever happens, and thus a clash occurs. Which leads them to question their own worth or to want to just fire everyone. This aspect of personal leadership growth takes the most time to overcome.

The last challenge area is that of plain old organizational trivialities such as the e-mails, the phone calls, the reports that need to be filled out. These are a necessary part of everyone's job in every business every day. While for some jobs it's only about 15 percent of the workload, for other positions it's about 50 percent. Regardless, it needs to get done for an organization to accomplish its workload. This is where our internal folks struggle the most. They just don't get it done. They don't see it as a priority. Some see it as "women's work" and feel it's a waste of their talent. They mostly refuse to do it, which becomes their biggest barrier to career advancement. However, after a lot of coaching "Dutch uncle" style, they come around and eventually get to a point of reconciling these issues.

Even with these challenges, we have terrific managers who have been able to overcome their obstacles and have attained high leadership positions. I saw it as one of my key responsibilities to make sure the organization develops its leadership pool just as big corporations do. The job of a senior leader is to groom the next generation of talent. The difference at Homeboy is that the task is taller and the resources limited. We've made a special effort to seek foundation support to provide resources for this training. One foundation took the risk with me to develop a miniversion of the leadership training program I received as I was developing my skill set at Aramark—minus the negative ego aspects. Additionally, hiring an experienced, senior-level human-resource professional was instrumental in creating an environment where more people seek to become managers.

The effort to develop the management team that is partially composed of leaders with homie experiences requires time, money, and most important, a mindset the whole organization needs to take on. Our greatest struggle is in the blending of the inside and outside talent. When it works, you get a beautiful mix of many different talents with everyone leaning in on their strengths to deliver the mission. When I talk to our leaders about teamwork, how each of us fits in, I often use the metaphor of a baseball team. Everyone on the field has a particular talent for their position and when each of the talents comes together in a cooperative way, then we will be successful. While the third baseman might want to be the pitcher, it's best if he plays his position and lets the pitcher do what he is best at. Thus, the case manager with deep, lived experience has better insight into client challenges than the teacher in the curriculum department. Likewise, the finance manager has a better sense of how much money we have left to hire trainees than the navigator who wants to bring on three more clients right away.

The leaders grown from within are extremely focused on the mission and do everything possible to help a client. However, at times, these leaders also view the outside professionals as less committed because they don't see the issue the same way or they put limits on what we can do. Likewise, when the outside professional puts a tremendous amount of hard work into providing sound processes and structure to work from—which in the end, helps our clients greatly—it becomes demotivating and frustrating when leaders with homie experiences work outside the system. What makes the situation even more problematic is that often the homie gets promoted more quickly, even though they didn't do a good job of staying within the rules and only sporadically completed their workplace tasks of e-mails, callbacks, and such.

This dynamic of the struggle between insiders and outsiders, or those with lived experience versus professional manager experience, is a cause of systemic inequity and by extension systemic racism—many times occurring as unintended consequences without people realizing it. For example, we have a small contract with the County of Los Angeles to provide case management services for the reentry population. This is a new program for the county and was a welcome relief in our view, since this was the first time in a long time that the county was willing to spend money with a community-based organization to achieve better outcomes for the reentry population. Homeboy currently employs eight case managers, and we asked the county to provide funding for all eight. The response was, Let's start with one, and if you do a good job, there will be money to fund others. This is frustrating, as I'd rather use donor funds to pay for other aspects of our program, not case management. We thought, "Let's 'play nicely' and go along with their request." This is a new program for the county, so they hired people to staff their new department, and they put together a county-approved plan on what good case management looks like. They required all community-based organizations to fill out a plan in their database. This meant that we needed to adjust our case management model (a model that has worked well for us over many years) to fit their construct. Our team would need to maintain the database for the county and for our internal system. Double the database work to get access to funds.

We managed to start with two case managers on the contract. We put two of our best people on this new effort since we wanted to demonstrate, at a high level, that we really do know how to help gang members turn their lives around. Many months later, money was tight, and we were still asking to bring the other six case managers onto contract. We were told no, because we did not perform well under the contract. When I heard this, I went back and spoke with my management team. I asked them how the trainees were doing on the caseload under the two county-funded case managers. They told me that the trainees were doing fine but were struggling to fill out all the fields in the database. Knowing that our case managers are former clients, it didn't surprise me that this would be a difficulty for them. They didn't refuse, they were just not as quick as was needed. I asked if we could supplement their efforts with a data entry clerk, and the county's answer was no, citing HIPAA rules.

What we have here is a person who went to college, received their master's in social work (MSW), then created a conceptual model of a case management that required a high need for a lot of data points. The model was based on working with the reentry population as clients and definitely was not created thinking of people with lived experience being the case managers and leaning into their strengths. It was developed by college graduates for college graduates. Our non-college graduates, our homies, who are terrific by all other measures at their jobs, feel like failures in this new realm. We have government bureaucrats wagging their fingers at us, saying don't ask for more case managers when your people can't even get this work accomplished. Their only measurement of success was whether or not the database got filled without consideration as to who was doing the work or the positive real-life client outcomes. Those officials are not incentivized to make a model that works for people with the kind of experiences that got them in trouble in the first place. They get their next promotion based upon the completeness of the database, and the outcomes of the clients are lost in translation.

Was it wrong that they required data? Absolutely not, but at what cost? If we as a society should be investing in people to move up the economic ladder, then these types of policies, these types of approaches need to be reimagined. In this county example, the questions should have been, "What is the minimum data needed, how do we capture meaningful client outcomes, and who will be maintaining the database?" This way, people with lived experiences will shine as case managers. It only takes willingness and leadership at the top of organizations to make this call.

At Homeboy, we openly talk about these challenges and the balance needed to have a blend of professionals with lived experiences and management experience, and the difficulties that come along with implementing it. We've openly and rightly taken on this challenge and are finding success. While there is no one correct set of answers or policies, we need to overinvest in developing our team to move ahead, and it's the role of everyone in the leadership to make this happen.

As the country reckons with how best to improve racial equity, I believe a main factor will be how to bring more people along—out of poverty—and into quality jobs that provide for growth up the economic ladder. What needs to be said clearly is, it's not good enough to just provide entry level (usually minimum-wage) positions, but a job that leads to something more substantive. To do so will mean overinvestment in terms of developing people's employment skills while they are working. A very proactive approach for people of color with the same type of lived experience is to provide the guidance, mentorship, and coaching. I suspect that the same factors that have presented a challenge for Homeboy will be the same factors other organizations face when endeavoring to truly push people up the economic ladder. Our hard-earned lessons should be models for other organizations that wish to take a similar path and work to bring about racial equity.

We are now midway through our efforts to achieve long-term sustainability. Of late, money has come in from newer sources who value how our organization has invested in the disenfranchised. Our management team is as strong as it's ever been, with a lot of great up-and-coming leaders grown from within. Our days ahead look bright.

I've met enough donors to know that the money will be there as long as they see that the next generation of leaders are stepping forward. I've now seen and experienced the two Americas up close and know that "people development" needs to be done differently.

Business needs to be done in a more socially conscious way. By sheer necessity Homeboy has found a way to accomplish this from within.

But will the rest of society take up that challenge?

Will overinvestment occur?

If I, with all my corporateness, can shift to truly see others, then other businesspeople can also.

If the rules of the game need to be broken, will others be willing to take the risk and do so?

CHAPTER 11

A NEW WAY FORWARD

The Homeboy way is a proven model, yet I find it so interesting how many "system" leaders come to visit, appreciate it, and congratulate us, then find ways to say why it can't work in their organization, institution, community, or city. I believe this stems from people complicitly operating in the system of society that benefits them and has made them successful. Many can't or are unwilling to see how this system, with its rules stacked up against our people (those who have been marginalized), needs disputation. They have too much of an unconscious resistance to changing the status quo, for they fear that it might negatively affect their own situation.

Father Greg had the courage to try something different and countercultural. Despite Homeboy's thirty-plus years of success as an organization, I still hear people claim that what we do won't last and can't work. I can only imagine how many naysayers there must have been at the beginning, when Father Greg first started this work. He knew there had to be a better way to help young men get out of gang life. So he innovated and disrupted the status quo. He stepped forward and took action. He wasn't willing to stand by and let death and gang violence destroy so many lives.

His innovation wasn't starting businesses with homies; it was moving himself and many, many other people to the margins to be in kinship with the demonized and forgotten. What he has demonstrated, has proven, has "shined a light" on, is that through the action of love, kinship, and community, people can truly change. This lies outside the American Dream way of thinking. It lies outside most systems by which America helps the poor because it lies outside people's comfort zone of hanging out only with their own tribe. Such a bold system chips away at the usual goals of more stuff and more status. The way forward is not to pursue the American Dream via a meritocracy with all the false incentives and nonexistent bootstraps. The way forward pursues the Homeboy vision: offering love, encouragement, and support that will make a lasting difference to our society.

It is a privilege and an honor to see and bear witness to people incredibly changing their lives over a twelve-to-eighteen-month period. How they come to love themselves and positively move their lives forward. Such transformation is miraculous, of a divine agency.

It's beyond disappointing that after this miracle takes place and homies are ready to leave our program, only a minimum-wage job awaits them. Not a living-wage job, not a job that has steady hours, not a job with upward mobility, not a job with good health benefits. If they do happen to get a minimum-wage job, it's certainly not the sort of job we'd envision for our own children to have for the rest of their lives in the America we live in. Thus, lifelong poverty awaits the people who successfully move through the Homeboy program, cutting ties to gang life and developing good life skills. For all the incredibly hard and painful work our people have done for themselves, society says that they remain unemployable.

The different realities and lived experiences born from the Two Americas was still eating away at me. I wasn't sure what to do about it. However, I began to focus on this issue: the failure to provide an adequate number of jobs with upward mobility that pay market-based wages is a core weakness of our society. For those who have transformed their lives—just as society wanted them to do—there really is no landing place for them to live with meaning and security. As Homeboy looks to the future, it has become apparent that we and our broader community must continue to cocreate the system changes that are so desperately needed. Together, we are the change agents leading the new way forward. The Homeboy 2030 vision is an expansive community of kinship that stands with, heals, and invests in those who have a history of gang affiliation and incarceration. There is a way forward that reimagines society's broken systems that perpetuate the generational cycles of poverty, trauma, racism, inequity, and recidivism. The Homeboy community has innovated one such model and has demonstrated an incredible return on investment for society.

I have learned, over my several years in this community, that the people working in our Homeboy social enterprises are just as valuable and competent as workforces in corporate America. I have seen for myself that the business managers in our social enterprises, who were once clients, are just as talented as the managers who worked for me in my big corporation. By talent alone, these managers should be highly employable and making more money. If not for their histories, they'd get those comparable for-profit jobs. We, as a non-profit organization with social enterprises, cannot pay market wages and thus, our very talented managers are only able to eke out a living.

We worked hard to accomplish the mission of our social enterprise businesses running as effectively as for-profit businesses, despite the amount of labor we have in each. We figured out a way to provide more workplace therapy opportunities for our clients without compromising the quality of our products and services that draw in customers. Our customers come to us not just because we are a nonprofit who does "good work" but because we have products and services they want.

As I think about Homeboy from the $6MDM point of view, I see that we have a great brand, successful businesses, a solid workforce, and great managers. Taken together in the for-profit world, Homeboy would be considered "investable." Given that Homeboy has the attributes of being investable and an ever-growing number of people who can and want to be employed, the question is how to find the investments? Who would invest in a set of nonprofit businesses? A significant amount of my time at Homeboy is dedicated to increasing fundraising capacity, and I've come across a fair number of very high net-worth donors. A few of them have said to me, "Tom, we like Homeboy and will continue to keep donating, but I have a lot more money. If you ever come up with a business in which I can put my capital to work, let me know." Each time this was mentioned to me, I thought about how to go about tapping into this much needed resource.

In many ways I'm "old school." I will not take other people's money without darn well knowing that I will be effective and successful with it. On the flip side, Homeboy has been around for thirty years and built a reputation of doing the work to help gang members transform their lives. Homeboy's model is proven and "investable" by all measures. However, raising money under the Homeboy umbrella to run and grow businesses requires a different pact with donors and investors. While deep down I knew we had the right business dynamics to be successful, the cost of failure at Homeboy is unmeasurable as compared to that in the for-profit world. Suppose we take the money and the business didn't work out. How would that "play" in the donor world? Would they lose confidence and pull their support altogether? At the same time, many of these would-be donors and investors understand business risk. Most have been part of "angel" or "venture" funds, where just one of every ten investments pays out. I understand business investments. In my last eight years at Aramark, my team and I made more than forty acquisitions of companies and sold some as well. The capital for these acquisitions came from either raising money as a public company in the stock market or through private equity ownership. Either way, we knew that to acquire a business we needed to demonstrate—in a financial model—that we would achieve a high rate of return.

Following the Private Equity (PE) model means to purchase a business with only 20 percent down as the purchase price, borrow the rest of the money (meaning take on debt), operate the heck out of the business so that the debt can be reduced, and then sell the business for a higher purchase price. That's when investors get paid. By doing this, you can earn three to five times your money invested. A brilliant return.

Following the Venture Capitalist (VC) model means taking investment money to grow your business. The caveat is that you are taking on fellow investors who become co-owners. So, when you need more money, they will own more of your business. This leads to them wanting to grow the company quickly so that they can sell their investment to somebody else for a quick profit. Mostly, VC money isn't in it for the long haul.

Either way, both models put a premium on stripping the entity down to its bare bones to maximize short-term profits, and because of this, the employees are very much an afterthought. In fact, employees are viewed as expendable and interchangeable. The challenge I've always faced is the tension between how to build a great company for the shareholders *and* its employees—at the same time. The investment world values top talent ($6MDM type skill set) but doesn't value frontline employees and is allergic to the notion of providing long-term employment. To make earnings happen, particularly in a non-technology business, you need to be leaner and move on quickly from people who do not have a high-value skill set. When ownership is focused solely on holding a company for a short period of time, they totally abdicate their responsibility and role of being good corporate citizens. Rather, they see the employer-employee societal pact as a quaint, "old fashioned" notion.

All this rubbed me the wrong way. I felt there could be a different way of looking at capitalism and investment capital that would be more beneficial for the workers of the business. What gave me confidence in this notion was the many family-run businesses I've seen over the years. Many of these were multigenerational and very successful. A strong attribute of these was the long-tenured workforces that they were able to retain. The investment world looks at these types of companies and sees underperforming assets. Their return on invested capital or their return on net assets are not in the top 25 percent of all similar companies. While this may be true for a year or a period of time, I've seen quite a lot of wealth creation occur for these family owners over a long period of time. So, this is in part my template as we push forward to do business differently. It's about achieving long-term financial returns while simultaneously creating employment and economic opportunities for a larger number of people.

Specifically, as you acquire businesses, if you are willing to expect a lower return on your money, say three to five percent, you can have a company that is employee-focused *and* successful over the long haul. With a lower expectation of return, there will not be a rush to sell the company to liquefy the investment. By not having a prescribed "exit strategy" upfront, the management team is given the freedom to make the right decisions for the long-term health of the business.

The way forward is to build businesses for the long term. Long-term employability, long-term profitability, long-term impact. This can all be accomplished as long as the investors are willing to accept a *modest* return on their money—call it a societal return or public-value return—not meager, not piggish, just a fair amount. Doing this is straightforward. Many people know how to build or acquire businesses, and I believe there are people (donors and investors) out there willing to accept a lower rate of return to accomplish a societal goal. The innovative part is to marry this investment model with a specific mission. At Homeboy, that mission is to provide good jobs for our graduates. Using investment capital to employ the unemployable into upwardly mobile jobs that pay market-based wages will have a monumental impact on our society.

Recently, we created a new legal entity called the Homeboy Ventures and Jobs Fund. This entity seeks to raise fifteen million dollars of investment capital that will be used to support and allow existing Homeboy businesses to grow and to fund the acquisition of new Homeboy social enterprises. So far, in a short period of time, we have raised nearly half the money and look to finish funding phase one within a year.

We hope to define a new slice of capitalism—let's call it Economic Equality Capitalism. This slice brings quality jobs to the most demonized and forgotten population in our country. Economic Equality Capitalism uses private capital to create economic opportunities for those who have lived in a system that promotes economic and racial inequality.

The government can do only so much. They set up enterprise zones (which is a good thing), workforce centers, and training-based tax incentives. Most of these programs are only halfway effective, but they make politicians feel good about talking about them. At the end of the day, businesses need to be created and successfully run to enable sustainable job creation. The way to do this is through the private sector. Up until now, there really hasn't been much capital invested into businesses that will meet these goals. The reason is that the criteria have just been to make money.

Yet it is possible to make money and employ the unemployable. This may not be a new idea, but it is an idea that works, and the proof is Homeboy. You don't have to go any further than to look at any of our social enterprises. Homegirl Catering is a business that was launched out of the training business of the Homegirl Café. Here we have a business that is led, operated, and grown by the women who have been promoted from within. This business is close to one million dollars in annual sales and yields a healthy profit margin. The catering customers range from law offices to political fundraisers, from private dinners to large weddings. The business has the ability to double in size but needs investment capital to make it happen. Another success story is that of Homeboy Silkscreen and Embroidery. We not only sell Homeboy branded apparel but also produce personalized clothing for other companies. This business does close to two million dollars a year and produces a slight profit margin while providing steady market-based wages for our Homeboy graduates. Both these businesses are fully run and operated by people who would have very few job prospects in the "outside world." They provide solid employment and a place to improve the lives of our people and the lives of the children of our people. How much could these businesses grow if we invested into them? Could we double the number of quality jobs by deploying investment capital? The answer is most certainly *yes*.

Another business, Feed Hope, is a newer one we created as part of a pandemic pivot within a three-week timeframe. This business was invented and incubated by the Homeboy Bakery and Café teams. At the beginning of the pandemic, the teams saw that we had a lot of food in our storage rooms, and they knew many people in our community were food insecure. They asked us in management if they could make meals with this food to feed the poor. The answer was a quick yes, and once others in the community found out about this program, we had donors calling us up to donate more money so that we could produce more meals. This led to gaining a contract with the County of Los Angeles to feed seniors who no longer had access to group food kitchens. From there, two of our board members got involved and raised more than four hundred thousand dollars for us to produce more meals and to grow this business into a free-standing operation. In just four months, Feed Hope has provided three hundred thousand meals to the poor and created sixteen new jobs. We believe this could be a three-million-dollar new business for Homeboy, providing seven hundred fifty thousand meals and creating quality jobs for our folks. And, it was born from within.

Think about the multiplier effect these types of business investments have. That by working in these businesses, our people are earning a decent wage; they have company-paid benefits and company-paid health insurance, nestled within a therapeutic healing community. Payroll taxes are paid; state and federal taxes are paid. Our people go from being a financial "burden" on our society to contributing members of our society who empower and create sustainable economic growth in the communities they live and work in. There was a study conducted in 2014 by the Mathematica Policy Research organization, which shows that for every payroll dollar earned by our target population, there is a $2.23 benefit to our society. Think about that in light of the Homeboy business payroll. Our current annual payroll is three million for those who work in our social enterprises. That means we will produce a "hard cost" savings to society of more than six million dollars this year.

Today, our total annual revenue across all our social enterprise businesses is seven million dollars, and we employ 120 people. With the fifteen-million-dollar investment from the Homeboy Venture and Jobs Fund, we believe we can double the size of our business over the next five years and in doing so, produce another 250 quality jobs *while* simultaneously producing a collective eighty-million-dollar savings for society. Pretty good payback on fifteen million dollars of invested capital. For you private-equity types, that's more than five times cash-on-cash. Darn impressive. It's what I call Economic Equality Capitalism done the Homeboy way.

Over the past few years, it's become in vogue to talk about "social impact" investing. Unfortunately, the term has become overused and not very impactful to our society. The large PE (Private Equity) funds and even foundations are leveraging the fact that many good-hearted people would like to have their money used in a way that is socially conscious. So they created these "social impact" and "green investing" funds. These fund creators are for the most part taking in this money and investing in businesses that are either "sin free"—no guns, no tobacco, no gambling, etc.—or environmentally friendly. While there is nothing wrong with investing in these types of companies, it's not an authentic social impact insomuch as they don't go to the root cause of economic and racial inequality within the systems of today's society. Even more problematic is that the fund promoters are still using their same investment criteria of high returns and are still looking for short-term gains, thus perpetuating the situation where employees are an afterthought within these companies. They are not investing in Homeboy-style social enterprises that are providing real jobs for the poor. They are not investing in businesses whose goals are to create career growth opportunities so that people can earn, at minimum, a living wage. Worst of all, they have these good-hearted investors believing that they can still earn a high return on their dollar by investing in these pseudo-social-impact funds, giving the impression that social-impact investing comes at no cost. I know you can't serve two masters—mammon and God. You cannot help your fellow American by focusing only on the accumulation of wealth.

The path forward I'm talking about is not complex. It's as simple as investing in businesses that provide economic opportunities to people who have not been given a fair shot before. This investment is not hard to make; it just takes the willingness to not fall into the trap of "maximizing shareholder value" by dictating that it either produce high yields or it needs a turnaround. The mindset needs to be financial returns *and* employment stability. Let's put our best business minds to use in creating companies with huge employment returns as opposed to creating companies with huge financial returns as the priority. Let's create businesses to reverse the decades-long legacy of economic and racial inequality. Let's create businesses that invest in people who are just beginning to see life bloom before them.

Let's create businesses the Homeboy way.

How do we get other business leaders and investors to follow suit? How can we convince the elites to change their attitudes and move into action? We need a mindset shift. We need to break from the old norms.

I see the path forward. I can taste it. I can smell it. And yet I fear that it is so far away. There are so many who need help right now. This dream could evaporate like a mirage on the horizon. Honestly, I vacillate between elation in knowing the path forward and anger that society will continue to not invest in this population that so desperately needs change.

CHAPTER 12

AS I WRITE THIS BOOK, PART 1: ANGER

As I write this book, it's April 2020. This country, our cities, states, and the world are in the middle of a pandemic. The COVID-19 virus is causing great harm to our society. It is in times of crisis that you see people either step up and step forward, or you see the worst of people come out. I want to share some business examples that indicate why I'm on a mission to do business differently. Homeboy Industries is a twenty-million-dollar organization. Six years ago, I convinced the board of Homeboy Industries to begin a banking relationship. Up until then, all it did was deposit money; we had no credit-borrowing facilities at all. Now we have a credit line of two million dollars that helps us greatly. Our yearly donations come in seasonally and we are able to tap that credit line to keep payrolls steady throughout the year. We were given a dedicated banker and believed they would be a steady partner in good times—and in bad.

On March 27, 2020, the federal government put out the Cares Act, a two-trillion-dollar economic stimulus bill, in part to enable nonprofits and small businesses with fewer than five hundred employees to maintain their payroll for the next two months. The goal was to mitigate a mass number of people being laid off or furloughed and becoming unemployed. After the announcement of the Cares Act, we contacted our banker. For two weeks we worked with them on the application and qualification requirements so that when the portal opened, we'd be ready to act fast. For us, this was critical because so many of our staff, our management team, and former clients live paycheck to paycheck—on the edge of financial insecurity.

Without a Homeboy job and paycheck, it's common for our folks to immediately begin feeling desperate and alone. Homeboy provides this security for them. Our strategy at an organizational level was to keep funding our payroll for at least the first two months while looking for donor support to help cover subsequent months, should the crisis last that long. A key aspect of making and being comfortable with this decision was understanding the rules and regulations behind the Paycheck Protection Program (PPP), a key component of the Cares Act and a conditional forgivable loan. Our bank assured us that they would be able to process the loan for us.

As soon as the federal government announced the April 5, 2020, PPP portal application open date, we worked with our banker twice a day. In these conversations, we were assured that we'd be near the top in line and get access to the dollars. On Friday, April 3, 2020, other banks opened their application portals. Our bank said, "Hold off. They don't have all the information correctly situated. Wait until Monday morning."

Over the weekend we kept checking our bank's portal, which never opened to the public. On Sunday, April 5, 2020, the bank's CEO issued a press release saying they were not going to participate in the PPP as expected. He further explained that they received only one-third of the funds they expected, or *ten billion dollars*, which was already sold out. Their reason? They claimed "regulatory oversight," which is stringent because of this bank's past misdeeds. What they said they needed was for the regulator to loosen up the oversight so they could serve more small businesses. Here we are, waking up Monday morning, ready to send in our application, and realize that our bank is not going to be there for us in a time of crisis, at a time when we need our bank the most. They pretty much said that they couldn't do anything for us at this time.

I called up our local contacts at the bank, ready to yell and argue. Within the first thirty seconds of the phone call, I was stunned to hear the sorrow in the voices of our contacts at the bank, knowing that they were turning their back on Homeboy, many other small businesses, and many other nonprofits. They had no answers. They couldn't tell us what the next step should be. When I asked, "Should I go look for another bank?" one said, "You've got to do what you've got to do." I hung up, still angry but feeling that they had been put in this tough position.

All day long, our senior team and board scrambled to find a new banking relationship. Most banks said no, that we had to be an existing client. Near the end of the day, a board member called a bank that was civically minded, who committed to providing us the PPP loan. The more I thought about it, I saw clearly what had been going on. The CEO of our original bank knew that they were under stricter regulatory oversight than all the other banks. They used the PPP as an issue to pry away deeper oversight, using small businesses and nonprofits as pawns in their "game of chicken" with the regulatory agencies. Would they get less oversight and thereby be able to make more loans? Or would the regulatory agencies stick firm?

I know how it plays out in these board rooms on Wall Street. Bankers sit back and game-theory the scenarios. They do their chess moves, they work on what would be best for them and their shareholders long-term. What's forgotten in this equation is what's best for their customers. In a time of national crisis, our bank could have done it differently. What they chose to do was to say that they had run out of asset cap for loaning more money to small businesses and nonprofits. But what they're really saying is this: They want to reserve their assets to ensure they can serve their bigger and most profitable customers. They're going to work for small businesses and nonprofits only if the government allows them to grow their asset cap and get off of regulatory oversight. They used small businesses and nonprofits as pawns.

The other action they could have taken was to simply say, "Listen, we know we're in a worldwide pandemic. We know the American economy is at stake. We know we have small businesses and nonprofits that count on us. We're going to forgo the loans we make for profitable customers and make sure we stand with the smaller businesses who are the backbone of the American economy." They may not have made more profits on that; their short-term earnings may have been hurt, but they missed the chance to show moral courage by standing up and saying, "There's a greater good at work here than just straight-line profits of a company down the line." I bring up this story because the bank probably made the same decision many of the other banks and big corporations would make in the same situation. They are all centered around shareholder equity, governance, oversight, and not around societal good.

We can do business in a different way. We need to set our priorities. What do we stand for? What's our commitment to our customers? What's our contract with society? How do we become good citizens, good *business* citizens in our society? In a time of national crisis, this bank had a chance to do all that, but instead they chose the way they've always operated. That's the problem with how capitalism often works out today. Misplaced priorities and the greed of individuals at corporations cause imbalances in society rather than use the system's strengths to make things better.

This is an example of how our society's style of capitalism has not worked. Homeboy, as an organization, was marginalized by a big bank in order for the bank to meet their profit-driven objectives. Luckily, we were "connected enough" to make a few phone calls and get another—importantly, LA-based—bank to step in and help. The lesson here is that we had "elites" on our board, who could call other "elites" to help us out. We knew the rules, how to play the game, and had some access to the game. What about all those other organizations who are doing good work, those who were left behind? They didn't have anyone fighting for them. We strive for awareness at Homeboy as well as action. Sometimes you need to ignite the anger in folks to awaken a new view.

As I write this book, there are more than twenty million people unemployed due to the closing of the economy and other structural failures this pandemic has exposed. I've long known that in a good economy, our people are the last ones to be employed. In other words, only when there are no jobs left to fill will an employer consider hiring a felon. In a bad economy, our people will be the first ones out of a job and will be unemployed the longest. These are the statistics on the macro level, but on the micro level, it's about the challenges of living, breathing human beings. The person who now has to struggle to put food on the table and to pay rent. The person who will have a longer gap in their work history and will have to answer more questions about their background. In the corporate America of my past—in the old days of companies being responsible to the community—many times when we had to lay people off, we used "unwritten" criteria when deciding whom to let go. We tried to make these individual decisions based on their situation in life. Could they get another job easily? Did they have support systems? How many people depended on them? The folks who had it the hardest would be the last ones laid off. But nowadays, the corporate world is so wrapped up in rules, regulations, employment policies, and labor laws that most of the time it comes down to last-in, first-out when deciding whom to lay off.

I write this with total clarity, for I've been fortunate to have witnessed life, oppression, successes, and rationales from many different perspectives. When I was young, I had a group of friends, some of whom were from upper-middle-class families and others who were from poor families. I started out in life with no privileged advantages—other than being a white male. But back then, being a white guy from a lower-middle-class family meant my advantage was being male. I was neither demonized for my race nor given a leg up as a result of my race—both were neutral for a white guy in a white society. I worked my way up the economic and class ladder. Throughout my professional life, I was able to peek in and experience a bit of the life of the super elite. Now I've come full circle to work with the poor and demonized. I've come to understand how the rich *view* those in poverty and how the poor *experience* poverty. Especially how very differently the concepts of the American Dream and meritocracy are understood between those of the Two Americas—it's the greatest gap I've ever seen.

In my corporate career, I was fortunate to attend board meetings of Fortune 100 companies. I met many Fortune 100 directors and was able to learn and observe their behavior. I heard how they see the world. I would come away astonished at how they thought they knew more than government leaders and how they saw the labor force as pieces on a chess board to move around. I met many of the top leaders of private equity companies and saw the glee they had at their success. Yet they never reflected on the human cost that came with those successes. They lived under this notion that people could easily gain employment elsewhere if they were let go. Very rarely did anyone speak up against this notion. I was a participant in over-the-top wasteful and gluttonous spending. I saw firsthand how the ego drives self-serving decisions to the detriment of doing what's right for the betterment of society. I heard their views on all sorts of political issues—which were of the right-wing sort of fare. While at these meetings, I knew my place was that of a dutiful executive who took their orders and laughed at their jokes. I would come home feeling thrilled at being so near the epicenter of power—but I knew something was amiss.

In my naivete, I pushed to the side that voice whispering, *Foul*; I behaved in a manner I thought was good or in line with my upbringing. I started to think that I needed to be more like them, to believe in their views—but I wasn't sure. I now know that little voice inside me was speaking the truth, that the gut instinct that something was amiss was right on. Looking back, I remember feeling increasingly like an outsider trapped in hallowed environments.

Now I see people lining up to tell investors that they can make money while investing in low-income communities. Really? I can't think of anything in the financial realm that is as immoral as this. If your goal is to help these communities and make a difference, why not just put the money to use—with no expectation of a return? Since when does it pass the smell test that you can make money off people who are struggling to survive?

We at Homeboy often receive solicitations from these fund managers who are aggregating money to do social-impact investing. To me, they are just hucksters looking for a different angle from which to make investment-fee money from poor people and organizations who serve them. They are promising a 10 percent return on investment and are targeting faith-driven investors. These types of guys are ruining the market for those of us innovating with modest investment instruments. They set the expectation in people's minds that you can make healthy profit returns by providing seed capital to poor communities. I most emphatically say that you cannot. You can make a small profit, but not like the returns they are talking about. To do so, you are not really creating quality jobs. You are mostly doing real-estate investments and waiting for the neighborhoods to turn over. It's very disingenuous.

In my time at Homeboy, I've had a chance to meet famous people from all different walks of life. From famous Hollywood types to royal families from a variety of countries; from high-ranking elected officials to businesspeople from top corporations; from Wall Street's top investor experts to white-shoe law firms; from top-notch business consultants to high-ranking religious leaders. I've had a chance to observe how they react to our trainees: some are moved, while others remain in the mode of lecturing us about life. A common failing of famous people is their belief that they have all the answers. Visitors of Homeboy fall into two groups: those telling us what needs to be done and those willing to listen and learn. Very few of the famous are in the listen category. I've sat in Father Greg's office, held captive in a lecture by a guest about where our folks went wrong. However, it's a real gift when we run across the very famous who just sit back, listen, and absorb. I salute those and thank them for their compassion.

Most famous people come in ready to tell us what is wrong and what needs to be done. However, by the end of the visit, our people have loved them unconditionally and managed to bring most into our fold. Only a few stick to their own views and don't ever contribute. I often wonder about these folks. Why couldn't we break through their hardened hearts? Why don't they offer help? Was it that they saw something too close to the truth of their lives—that they really didn't get to where they are all by themselves? That they had a mentor or someone who gave them a second chance but are unable to admit it? These people have such abundance, and yet they hold back. Why?

I've been at the margin for the last eight years, working with the poorest and most despised people in our society—and I still find myself at times feeling like an outsider. I hear how they come at issues that relate to making their lives better. Often, behind their experiences with those who have let them down, I see the invisible force of a racialized system. In my opinion, they are used as pawns in political fights to win over voters. Yet when the fight is won, there really isn't any effort put into making the lives of the poor better. I see our folks place their trust in politicians and other renegers over and over again—because there is no better alternative.

I see from the poor the reliance on government programs and the expectation that the government will take care of them. The safety net of welfare expenditures is meant for them—to help them through all the trauma they have experienced. Yet these dependencies just cement their status to always be in the lowest caste of our society. They don't want to stay there, and they don't want to keep depending on the government. No matter how hard they work to climb their way up, they just can't seem to get out of the hole. I've had many conversations with people who know their reliance on government programs is not a good thing, but they have no alternative. I want to give a speech at each of the Democratic and Republican National Conventions about the plight of the poor, because neither party is addressing any of these issues. How can it be that voters don't hold them accountable? Now is the time for change, but little is said or discussed other than what is necessary to get their tribe elected. This makes me angry. Can Homeboy and a few other organizations really be the only ones making meaningful change? Isn't that what God would want us to do? In the vernacular of business, wouldn't He want us to win together and not have losers? In the vernacular of government, wouldn't He want us to prioritize "reverse cherry-picking" so that *everyone* is lifted up? We've had mass protests for many months, yet very few policy changes are happening.

Today, I vacillate between anger and hope.

What makes me angry is the way society forgets about the poor. How can so many people just go about living their lives while millions of people are barely able to make it in our society today? I'm angry that so many "decisions" about how to help the poor come from those in ivory towers whose plans and policies have very little applicability to practical life, to meaningful system change, or to the lived experiences of those they seek to help. A good example of this was during the last few years of the Obama administration, when they decided that building transitional housing was not the right way to go, that it was better to have permanent low-income housing. I'm not here to dive into that debate, but it's obvious to anyone who has worked with the poor and homeless that both are needed. So, the federal government took away all incentives for transitional housing and now we have no new desperately needed facilities coming online.

The Federal Workforce Development Program is another example. In order to access funds to help people being released from prison to transition back into society, you must work with the individuals prior to their being released. Sounds good in theory, but most inmates don't take job certification skills seriously while they are incarcerated—they are forced to do it. However, in our experience, once they are on the outside and find out how hard it is to get a job being an ex-offender, they show up at Homeboy looking for help. We, of course, help them but are prohibited from using any federal funds because the program's requirements don't line up with this known pattern of behavior. When we talk with the contracting officers, they admit that this is a mistake but say they can't do anything about it. Again, here is policy created by the powers that be who were not incarcerated themselves and who don't bother to come to the margins to understand the struggles of those transitioning from being "freed."

I'm angry at all the politicians who come to Homeboy to pose and have their pictures taken with Father Greg and the homies. Very few of them enact legislation or funding opportunities to community-based organizations. I've always been curious as to why more doesn't happen. They see the need but in the end, shift their priorities. The poor are not really a voting bloc or a contributing one. A number of years ago, there was excess money in the city from a real estate development project. Organizations were asked to submit a proposal outlining how they would use the money if awarded the funds—we did. We asked for money to provide more tattoo removal services for our clients. We were not awarded the two hundred thousand dollars. We lost out because our local councilman had a pet project to bring a trolley down one of the main avenues in Los Angeles. A few years later, that councilman was arrested by the FBI for taking bribes from real estate developers. I'm angry. There have been a few elected officials who have done the right thing, who have helped us out even though it didn't serve their reelection chances. To those, I'm deeply grateful.

I'm angry over the fact that when I turn to investors, their funds come with expectations of large returns. In these days of being more "woke," we see a lot of headlines about corporations supporting the movement of racial justice who pledge to correct racial inequities within their organizations. Yet when we approach so many of these organizations to do business with our social enterprises, they always look for the low-cost supplier. A good example is our Homeboy Electronics Recycling company. We take electronic waste and recycle it, employing our homies to make this work happen. When we ask big corporations to pay one hundred dollars for each pickup, they say no, knowing that a competitor will do it for free. Even when we point out that our competitors send components downstream to disreputable suppliers—more than likely using child labor in Asia—they turn a blind eye. Where are the ethics of "Do the right thing" and "Take care of your own"? If we don't employ these guys, they will have no alternative but to return to the streets—back to the only means of survival they know—instead of picking up electronic waste. Corporate America doesn't often see its obligation to help out. Rather, they hide under the "free markets" concept instead of truly pulling back the curtain, owning their part, and doing something to change it.

My anger is around anyone "in power" who is not putting plans in place to help the poor. It is with society, the collective of all the leaders within government and corporations. Why was I chosen to get this insight? How do I do something about it? Should I shake the tree? Shake people into seeing how their inaction while holding powerful positions contributes to these injustices?

I'm hopeful that others might be able to see the goodness and value of the poor through my eyes. Hopeful that if society looks at the situation only a little bit differently, they can make a real difference. Hopeful in knowing that I've met so many very generous and kindhearted people, who lean into these problems of humanity with their time and their resources. Hopeful in knowing that by giving someone just a bit of love, they might be able to overcome the trauma they have suffered.

Anger can damage, but it can also supply the right kind of energy. My anger propels me forward. I have seen what happens at Homeboy, and it works. Society needs to wake up and support more efforts like the Homeboys of the world. My hopefulness is about bearing witness to the innate goodness of people. Putting efforts in place for action based on this goodness of people is the path forward.

We see all the time the damage that anger can do. New clients often come into our program just plain angry. Angry at the situation they find themselves in. Angry at the realization that their life has been nothing but turmoil. Angry at the police for the abuse they've experienced. Angry with how the criminal justice system has treated them. Angry that their family has abandoned them. Angry that their "homies" have led them astray. Angry at the racism they've had to absorb. Angry that they've had no chance to get a decent job. Angry at the inequities they have witnessed for years. Angry with themselves.

Our team understands this very clearly and works with the trainee to alleviate this anger through the facilitation of relationship building. This leads to more self-discovery and positive attachments, which are crucial for healing. These positive attachments lead the individuals to invest the effort required to move their lives forward, leaving the anger behind. Staying mired in anger will stand in the way of life transformation.

This point was expressed by James, a former client and now a Homeboy leader. We bring in a lot of visitors, believing that it's part of the duty to our mission to open our doors and show as many people as possible what we do. For some of these visits, we set up a roundtable forum to allow visitors a chance to dialogue with our team and hear about Homeboy firsthand. On one such occasion, the senior leadership of AT&T Communications was on site. James was there with a few of our other leaders who were once program participants. I can so distinctly remember when it came time for James to tell his story. He was sitting right next to the CEO and began telling his story in a slow and methodical way. As the story moved from childhood to being a teenager, a clear pattern emerged. At each pivotal moment, he described how angry he was with his situation. In those moments, you could see this anger reemerging in his body language. Not a violent anger, but a sad and hopeless anger. An anger born out of frustration. He wanted a different situation. Growing up, he didn't always understand why or how the deck was so stacked against him.

As I heard James's story, I was reminded of the thoughts and feelings I had reading Ta-Nehisi Coates's story. In his book *Between the World and Me*, Coates tells multiple stories of what it was like growing up as a black teenager in the Baltimore-Washington DC metro area. He recalls his fear, frustration, and anger. As I heard James's story, it was remarkably similar to the experiences of Coates:

I was pulled over by the [Prince George] County police, the same police that all the D.C. poets had warned me of. They approached on both sides of the car, shining their flashing lights through the windows. They took my identification and returned to the squad car. I sat there in terror. By then I had added to the warnings of my teachers what I'd learned about PG County through reporting and reading the papers. And so I knew that the PG County police had killed Elmer Clay Newman, then claimed he'd rammed his own head into the wall of a jail cell. And I knew that they'd shot Gary Hopkins and said he'd gone for an officer's gun. And I knew they had beaten Freddie McCollum half-blind and blamed it all on a collapsing floor. And I had read reports of these officers choking mechanics, shooting construction workers, slamming suspects through the glass doors of shopping malls. And I knew that they did this with great regularity, as though moved by some unseen cosmic clock. I knew that they shot at moving cars, shot at the unarmed, shot through the backs of men and claimed that it had been they who'd been under fire. These shooters were investigated, exonerated, and promptly returned to the streets, where, so emboldened, they shot again. At that point in American history, no police department fired its guns more than that of Prince George's County. The FBI opened multiple investigations—sometimes in the same week. The police chief was rewarded with a raise. I replayed all of this sitting in my car, in their clutches. Better to have been shot in Baltimore, where there was the justice of the streets and someone might call the killer to account. But these officers had my body, could do with my body whatever they pleased, and should I live to explain what they had done with it, this complaint would mean nothing. The officer returned. He handed me back my license. He gave no explanation for the stop.[31]

The anger that comes from being a victim of these types of indignities, violence, and injustice is understandable. Ta-Nehisi Coates's anger, James's anger—we all should be angry.

Listeners always become transfixed when our folks tell their stories. The AT&T CEO was definitely in this state when hearing something so real and visceral. The anger made sense to him. As James got to the point of the story where intense anger was present, he very calmly and thoughtfully paused. He

31. Ta-Nehisi Coates, *Between the World and Me* (New York: Spiegel and Grau/Random House, 2015).

talked about how he is a different person now and knows how to manage his frustrations and channel that energy into making a better life for himself and his family. Having been around a lot of high-powered CEOs, I'm accustomed to them having an answer for everything and dominating the room with their point of view. In the moments after James finished his story, this CEO quietly moved to a space of exquisite mutuality with James and embraced James for his unshakable goodness.

CHAPTER 13

AS I WRITE THIS BOOK, PART 2: RACISM

As I write this book, most of America is undergoing much turmoil in digesting the meaning and causes of racism that were on display during the murder of George Floyd. Meanwhile, a great number of other Americans have been and continue to be retraumatized by this and countless other incidents of police brutality and murder. This, combined with the forced isolation in response to the global pandemic of COVID-19, has made many people angry, fearful, depressed, and hopeless. These crises have put on full display the widespread racial inequities in our healthcare system, our economy, and our criminal justice system.

We know that racism exists. The question is, what are we as members of society to do about it? What are our roles? How do we create systematic change? Do we need to change the structure of our society or just work to change our attitudes? Do we need to "blow up" or "start over" with policing, healthcare, education—or just make reforms from within?

These and other necessary questions are heavy and profound. If we care about eliminating racism, we must work to seek understanding and answers. We must understand the past movements and learn from former leaders. We need to channel our collective anger and get to a place of healing. We must listen to one another and not let catch phrases trip us up or set us off. This is not a Left issue or a Right issue, it's an "us" issue. As we talk with one another, we need to respect the feelings and perspectives of others. We must confront ourselves and reflect on our lives.

Homeboy is a multiracial organization that successfully helps people transform their lives. We are 60 percent Latino, 20 percent Black, and 20 percent White. It's not unusual for me to be the only white person in the room. I say this only for context, for in my prior professional life, there were never more than 20 percent people of color in my immediate work setting. I listen to the best of my ability. In fact, over the years we have had many dialogues about racism. When clients come into the program, they are broken and full of anger—racial anger. All their lives, the educational system has let them down, the economic system has oppressed them, the criminal justice system has dehumanized them, and the healthcare system has never really existed for them. All their lives, racism has worked against them. Sticking to their race meant survival. For example, when in prison—with few exceptions—Blacks stay with Blacks, Latinos with Latinos, Whites with Whites. An ongoing task at Homeboy is to help all of our clients see people of another race as their brothers and sisters. To be in community with one another.

Our perspective is not to change the system but to help change individuals so that the system might eventually change.

Clients entering our program are full of racist attitudes. They come with anger from having served prison time or anger at the gang that wasn't there for them. They are angry that their family was not supportive. Angry at the injustices they suffered. Angry at being a victim—a victim of racialization—over and over again. And they are tired of being angry.

The Need for Self-Reflection

The consideration of racism has moved me to reflect on my own experiences. My recollections may not be accurate in every detail, but they still give me food for thought.

Our parents, through their words and actions, taught us to treat all people respectfully, regardless of their race. I never heard my mother or father use a racist word or phrase. This was remarkable considering all the influences around them. Mother grew up in Paterson, New Jersey, which is today as it was then, a densely populated city made up of over 35 percent African Americans and a poverty rate twice the national average. She lived on the side of town that had her going to a predominantly Black high school. Her father, my grandfather, was in and out of low-wage jobs his whole life. For a bit of time, he was a milkman and a bartender. He drank too much and would blame his situation on others, specifically "the Blacks." My father grew up in Montclair, New Jersey, which today—as it did back when he was a kid—has an upper-class feel and a ritziness to it. However, he grew up in the poor section, the area on the border of Orange, New Jersey. His section of town was a mix of Italian immigrants and Black families. His childhood friends were of all races.

Racist language and attitudes were prevalent during our growing-up years, but our parents worked hard to move us past those feelings and hatreds, to respect all people.

Our parents were part of the generation that helped move the country forward to reduce racism and help people come out of poverty. Our parents' role was to protect us from the ugliness and to build a better life for us. As their children, we are essentially the bridge generation who witnessed much change, but we were too young to be active participants. We came of age in a society that was becoming more open and inclusive. Which then leads to our children, who, being white, have not—up till now—had to deal with race issues and the speciousness of racism. I think of it this way: people of my generation are at least more likely to acknowledge that racism exists. This has carried into the next generation, which, especially in diverse urban areas, is quite aware of the problem. The challenge remains the same across generations: what actions to take to battle the systemic racism that is so tenacious over time.

When I worked in Lexington, Kentucky, on my direct-report teams were two African Americans, both greatly respected in our workforce. However, when we as a team would have meetings away from the office, I saw how they were treated differently in subtle ways—only because of the color of their skin.

Not too long ago, I had a conversation with a Homeboy donor who volunteers with us. She is Black, and it turns out she grew up in the Northeast as I did. She went to a top law school and has a six-year-old son. As she spoke of her fear about what life might look like for her son as he grows up, she became tearful. She is a highly educated woman in a successful law practice, and yet she has the same fears and concerns as the gang member who comes to us to change his life. Racism has no socioeconomic boundaries.

It is no longer enough to simply view oneself as "not racist." In Ibram Kendi's book *How to Be an Antiracist*, he defines an antiracist as "one who is expressing the idea that racial groups are equals and none needs developing, and is supporting policy that reduces racial inequity."[32] He says, "To be an antiracist is a radical choice in the face of [our] history, requiring a reorientation of our consciousness."[33]

Beyond the labels of "not-racist" or "antiracist," we, on an individual level, must look at our actions and attitudes and decide if they are oriented toward racial equity. The challenge with the first step is that many of us may work in an organization that has not thought this way before—or has even professed to be color neutral in their approach, which is not enough to get the whole way to racial equity. We must first contemplate our own actions and attitudes, then act to work from within the structures of our organizations to make change happen. This is a tall order, particularly for someone who works in a large corporation. As with most things, large shifts in direction and policies need to come from the top leadership team. Organizations that have developed a learning culture will be the first ones able to make the shift.

During my time at Aramark in the early 2000s, we had a corporate-wide initiative around talent acquisition and development. Being a decentralized service business, we knew that our overall business success was dependent on having excellent local leaders who were entrepreneurial with excellent management skills. We coined this initiative "the war for talent." By recruiting constantly for great leaders and developing many from within, we would achieve business success. A key tenet of the program was understanding that the management team needed to be as diverse at the teams they led. Because so many of the frontline positions were held by people of color and recent immigrants, we knew that needed to be reflected in the makeup of the leadership team. As is typical in a large organization that is results oriented, if you want to achieve a goal, you need to measure for results and hold people accountable. So, for a

32. Ibram X. Kendi, *How to Be an Antiracist* (New York: One Word/Random House, 2019), 24.
33. Ibid., 23.

span of the next several years, I and all the other senior executives were evaluated on our efforts to improve diversity among our management ranks as part of our annual review. In retrospect, that is, in today's terms, an antiracist policy led by the chairman. Over time these proactive efforts worked, and Aramark has consistently been recognized as a top company for workplace diversity.

Kendi also says, "Antiracism means separating the idea of a culture from the idea of behavior. Culture defines a group tradition that a particular racial group might share but that is not shared among all individuals in that racial group or among all racial groups. Behavior defines the inherent human traits and potential that everyone shares."[34] To see racism and take antiracist action, we must learn to separate these two constructs. For emphasis, let's state the opposite. Racism occurs when one is unable to separate culture from behavior and takes a person's behavior and applies it to an entire racial group, often to subordinate individually or institutionally.[35] One of Father Greg's strong points of view is that the criminal justice system—mostly police departments—responds to the behavior of a gang member without looking to treat the root causes of why young men join gangs in the first place. Father Greg travels the country to talk about Homeboy Industries and often finds himself on panel discussions in various cities to talk about "their gang issue." Always, when he comes home and talks about it, the opinion is remarkably the same—they are not looking for the root cause but are dealing with behaviors. It's easy to see how this leads to systemic racism in the criminal justice system. Homeboy's approach is to treat the *person* who joined the gang. We work with gang members, not gangs. We work to help the person heal from the complex trauma that led them to join a gang. Given that Homeboy has such a diverse population, one of our strengths is our culture. We lean into aspects of our various culture groups to help our people heal, grow, and develop healthy behaviors. Whether it's spirituality, family norms, cuisine preferences, the arts, or other traditions, they all factor together to help someone through the hard parts of transformation.

---

34. Ibid., 95.
35. US Civil Rights Commission, "Racism," https://academic.udayton.edu/race/01race/race08.htm.

Another of our fundamental beliefs is that *it's hard to hate someone you have a relationship with*. So, we make sure the Latino gang member works side by side with a Black gang member. We work hard not to allow the natural tendency to hang around people of your own culture, which occurs most often with new trainees. So when we see a few folks from similar cultures kicking it together, we make sure to break it up and move people along into a bigger, more diverse group. We are very culture conscious, but from a healing sense, we know all our folks have been victims of racial trauma, and our role is to help them through that realization.

Sometimes people confuse racism (defined earlier, with an emphasis on subordination and the racialized structures created as a result) with discrimination (unequal treatment based on group membership.)[36]

On an organizational level, Homeboy does discriminate. We choose the hardest of the hard cases to work with. We take on the people no other entity will work with. We turn away people who we feel can get a job on their own or when we feel another organization might be willing to work with them. So we—in the end—discriminate to work with people society has thrown away. We invest our time and resources in a way that helps to reverse the subordination of America's racialized ecosystem of violence so once our folks are healed and resilient, they have a fairer shot of having a more equitable life.

Our only chance at dismantling racial injustice is to be more curious about how it still exists today than worried about our comfort as we realize our contributions to it. If we were to offer ourselves some forgiveness for our part in racism, might we be willing see our role in absentmindedly fostering it? Once we become aware, then it's our obligation to act to change this dynamic.

Add a Pandemic

As of early July 2020, Homeboy Industries' doors had essentially been closed for fourteen weeks and counting. Back in mid-March, when the breadth of the

---

36. Rodolfo A. Bulatao and Norman B. Anderson, eds., "Prejudice and Discrimination" in *Understanding Racial and Ethnic Differences in Health in Later Life: A Research Agenda* (Washington, DC: National Academies Press, 2004), https://www.ncbi.nlm.nih.gov/books/NBK24680/.

worldwide pandemic was coming to realization, the state of California, and particularly Los Angeles County, implemented a stay-at-home order. While the county made this a recommendation, they also wrote in their stay-at-home order that gang rehabilitation programs were exempt from this and considered essential operations. We were lucky that a couple of other exemptions applied to us too, including our nonprofit status and having a social enterprise food-related business. Fortunately, we were able to keep our doors open but had to make sure everybody stayed safe. We chose to close our doors to the program side of what we do but continued to operate our bakery and café. That was a difficult decision. We knew the importance of the stay-at-home order and that our population was going to be among the most vulnerable. One, because of their underlying health conditions and, two, because they tend to live in more crowded conditions. Three, their loved ones are still out there working as essential workers too.

In making the determination to close our doors, we also realized that by not having our building open every day, we were removing what for many folks was their sanctuary. A place they could de-stress, work on their issues, including drug-abuse recovery. Also, it was an escape from gang and neighborhood.

As a co-leader of Homeboy Industries, after the first four to six weeks I was so proud of our team. We innovated. We made sure all our case managers and navigators called everyone on their client list multiple times a week. We had Zoom classes, Project Fatherhood classes, anger management classes, and AA and NA were still happening. We knew we needed to go overboard to keep reaching out, and that's what we did. Nevertheless, after five or six weeks we saw the stickiness we had with our trainees fading away. Increasingly, some were falling backward—into domestic violence situations, drug abuse, and running with their gang. In fact, over those weeks we had had seven people who were affiliated with Homeboy die from drug overdoses, gang violence, or being in the wrong place at the wrong time.

In mid-June, we decided to reopen our doors and began bringing people back slowly—at first, roughly 25 percent of the people we serve. We saw that we were losing our youth and not connecting with them as much. We needed a specific effort, a pandemic pivot, to create and sustain connection with our folks during this time of isolation. Key to our mission is to have relationships, and thus we needed to do things that would allow us to be together safely and not necessarily inside.

We organized a hiking trip for the first week of July. One of our directors, José, chose five or six homies that would go on the hike. We didn't leave on time; a couple of the younger guys couldn't get transportation to our office, so José had to pick them up. They hadn't eaten in twenty-four hours, so he stopped and got them breakfast.

These three guys are all under the age of eighteen and from rival gangs. They met up in county jail and stayed with each other in one room in the back of someone's house. The best part of their day was when they were able to come to Homeboy and talk to others. These young men are what we sometimes call wobblers. They wobble between the lifestyle that's almost preordained for them—running with the gang—and trying to change their life and do better. We drove out to the Angeles National Forest and set off on a hike up Echo Mountain. It's about a five-mile hike round trip and it rises to about one thousand feet in elevation. It's a moderate hike. The team we took hadn't hiked much before, but they were superexcited to take off and get there. These three young guys are like characters out of central casting. One is a tall, thin guy, another is a moderate-sized guy but chunky, and the third is even shorter and very thin. They've all got attitudes.

José led the pack with these three fellows while Eva, Samson, Jules, and I hung back at the end of the line. As we began the hike, we went over some safety precautions and took off in single file; then conversations ensued. The initial conversation concerned the length and difficulty of the hike. That day, we had June gloom in Los Angeles, so it was pretty overcast and cool. They couldn't see the tall mountain we were climbing as we made our way to the lookout. It wasn't until we got to the top and looked down that they realized how much they'd accomplished in that two-and-a-half-mile hike up the mountain to Echo Canyon. It was fun. At the top we stopped and sat down.

I had energy bars with me and handed them out, making sure everyone also got plenty of water. The smiles on their faces and sense of accomplishment in the air were incredible. They'd never been to the mountains before. This was only a fifteen-mile drive from Los Angeles. They'd never done a hike like that before either. They were kidding around, recalling how they didn't want to go any further, how they just wanted it to end. But there was a sense of accomplishment. On the way down we had more conversations. I was again in the back of the line, this time with a fellow named Jules.

Jules is an African American guy in his mid-twenties. What's amazing about having Jules on this hike is that about five months prior, we had almost terminated him from our program. While he was working in one of our social-enterprise businesses, he'd come in on his days off and hang out in the back of our facility, spreading rumors and talking smack. One day, a guy he was spreading rumors about came along and knocked him down. Jules got up and started fighting back. This is a big no-no. We have very little violence at Homeboy Industries. It's rare to have a fight like that happen. Our cultural norms dictate that if you're involved with violence, you need to leave, think about it, and tell us when you're ready for our program again.

The next day in council, we had a long debate about whether we should keep Jules in our program. Jules knew he had messed up. He reached out and sent text messages to a number of people. Father Greg was on one of his trips. The hotline works fast at Homeboy. Within a few hours, Father Greg knew the story and knew the point of view of our leaders. Do we give Jules an extra chance or do we draw this hard line that no violence is permitted? As we learned more of Jules's story and the changes he'd made already, we decided to give him a second chance. I thought it was interesting that José chose Jules to be on the hike with us that day.

On the way up the mountain with Jules, I was struck by how he seemed to be in a much better place emotionally and I learned about his goals and accomplishments. As we were talking on the way down, someone in front asked him, "What are you doing with yourself these days when you're not in the office?" He said, "I've been doing a lot of reading," which pricked up my ears. I said, "What are you reading these days?" He said, "I'm reading books about Martin Luther King and Malcolm X."

This is six weeks after George Floyd's murder, a few weeks after the many riots, protests, and peaceful marches coming out of the Black Lives Matter movement. I thought it was interesting, listening to his reading list in light of the current situation. As this situation has hit America, I've been trying to learn more too—watching more documentaries, reading more books, and I had just been reading Kendi's book *How to Be an Antiracist*.

In the section I just read, Kendi talks about Malcolm X. I know a lot of our guys have found Malcolm X; he was in jail for five years. That's where he began adopting the Nation of Islam philosophy. That's where his anti-White hatred came about. What I didn't know, as I read in Kendi's book, was that Malcolm X in 1964 left the Nation of Islam. He left because he realized they were being racist themselves—racist among themselves and racist toward other people. He went public with his realization in September of 1964 and was assassinated just a few months later. As Jules was telling me about his readings, I asked, "What do you think about Malcolm X and his assassination? Why do you think he was murdered?" I learned a lot from Jules in this discussion. We talked about the conspiracy theories as to why Malcolm X was assassinated; then Jules talked about some of his theories. We talked about Martin Luther King Jr. being assassinated and the conspiracy theories about his assassination too. I said, "Clearly, Martin Luther King Jr. was murdered. What group do you think was behind that?" He had a very considered answer. He wasn't just saying it was the government or the CIA, and he wasn't just saying it was the KKK. His answer was more of an understanding that there were a lot of people who didn't believe in Martin Luther King Jr.'s peaceful protest movement, and a lot of bigoted people out there who didn't want to see his philosophy succeed. That's why he thought they stopped him.

As I listened to Jules speak about Martin Luther King Jr. and about his understanding of Malcolm X, we hopscotched to the late rapper Nipsey Hussle. Jules shared how Nipsey was shot and murdered by his homie but that there was money behind that—as the guys say. What I came to really appreciate about being in kinship with Jules was this. Here's Jules, someone who's had an awful life. He's been in and out of jail and sees what's going on around him. He knows the racism that's around him; he knows the leaders he follows, how their lives were extinguished at a young age because of things they said. And yet, he takes this all in and is now in the mindset of focusing on what he's got to do to be successful. Focusing on what his dreams and goals are. His dream is to be a real-estate guy, buy property, run small businesses, buy other properties, and keep on growing. He wants a better life for himself and for his little daughter.

I'm not suggesting that he wasn't concerned about the George Floyd murder or wasn't frustrated over the assassinations of Martin Luther King Jr. and Malcolm X. But he chalked it up to understanding how life works, the behaviors of certain culture groups. He decided to focus on what he needed to do. As I left the hike that day, I thought a lot about that. Again, I think Homeboy helps by helping people deal with their wounds, anger, and frustration. Jules decided that his way to move his life forward was to walk a straight and narrow path. To get a better job and make good for his family.

A simple hike led to exquisite mutuality.

We need to realize that God is pulling us to the margins to be with the people who are the most demonized, forgotten, and oppressed. We are on the margins to be in kinship with them and to use our own God-given talents to aid in their transformation. These talents may lead to systemic changes or may lead to helping just one person. Either way, action must be taken. We also need to realize that a meritocracy doesn't work for these folks, that the capitalist system doesn't work for these folks, that our current leaders in state and local government don't have the solution. What works is moving to the margin in the community. What works is exquisite mutuality to heal mutually. What works is solving problems in a mission-driven and collaborative way. What works is investing in the poor with meaningful public goods and services.

Homeboy shines a light on the goodness of everyone. Homeboy stands in kinship with the oppressed so that the oppression will stop. Homeboy enables the "broken" to heal and transform their lives. Homeboy helps the unemployable become employable. The promise of Homeboy is that by moving to the margins with the forgotten, your life and their lives will be filled with joy.

I've learned so much about myself in terms of what preconceived notions I had about the poor and, in particular, about my own privilege of believing society needs to be color-blind. Society's structure needs to move beyond indifference to race to embracing policies that create equity for all races. I've also learned that people's beliefs and aspirations should be valued and respected, for we are all of one humanity with such different lived experiences and histories—and God loves all of us equally.

I don't know how to make large-scale societal changes. What I do know is what I've experienced here at Homeboy. That when you are in kinship with one person at a time, you realize there is no us and them, just us. In this way, incrementally, a movement is created—and we become the change.

My gut instinct is telling me—and the $6MDM inside me knows—that if the collective at Homeboy can innovate to create an equitable system, just imagine what the collective of *us* could do.

BREAK THE RULES: 55 BELIEFS, PRACTICES, AND ASSUMPTIONS WE ALL NEED TO CHALLENGE

I've lived my whole life in the mode of "don't break the rules." What my eight years at Homeboy have taught me is that people need to go out of their way to help people *and* that we need to do business differently. To do well in the marketplace while providing social value, we must break the rules. I've tried to highlight in this book the many rules we live by—particularly for those of us who work in for-profit companies—rules that should be done away with. In order to truly help individuals and to help ourselves, we must not be so rule-bound. We need to bust up the system, swim upstream, avoid herd mentality. We need to take a step back and truly understand our own role in society.

Another way of saying all of this is that unless we shake off our current way of going about life, there will be another generation of people lost in our society.

The rules I'm referring to are those barriers that exist within ourselves and in our society that keep the poor being poor; the demonized people, despised; and the traumatized people, suffering.

After fifty-plus years of living on God's green earth, I have finally learned something different: by being willing to put the individual above my own needs or the organization's needs, I can be part of a transformational process, and more people will be healed and equitized.

These are not written-down rules. They are the unspoken but agreed-upon beliefs, practices, and assumptions we all need to challenge.

The two biggest assumptions that need to be challenged are, first, that we who go about our everyday life in our own little bubble think it's none of our responsibility to get involved with the way society treats its poor. Or that because we are distracted by our own stressors, we think it's someone else's responsibility to be accountable to our fellow human beings. I want to shout from the rooftops that *it's all our responsibility* and it's really not that hard to do our part. The second big assumption is that society at large has the answers and already has the best available solutions in place to fix the systems of inequity. This is far from true, and to make a real difference, we need to break business norms, governmental norms, and societal norms.

I am no saint; I've made plenty of mistakes along the way and will still make errors going forward, but at least I am more aware now of the systems that keep people from leading better lives. I see something different now. I, the $6MDM, the tool of corporate America, was able to shed my armor to see and eventually step into my responsibility—what I believed to be a main purpose in my life—of creating an effective model of Racially Equitable Capitalism. I was the guy who thought he had figured it all out. I then became so very aware of how little I had figured out and how naive I was to think God wasn't with me the whole way.

Homeboy not only helps gang members move their lives forward but also helped a plain old middle-class son of an immigrant father and a poor mother, turned corporate executive and elite, living in the trappings of "success" and the Privileged America, see that a life in service of our Creator is the path forward. The real path forward—and along the way we need to break rules!

I'm not a deep thinker who comes up with new insights, nor do I profess to understand the complete historical significance of many of these topics, but I'm learning, and I endeavor with my whole heart to do what is right and just. I'm a practitioner who has seen both sides of society, both sides of the Two Americas, and I see a path forward.

Here are the rules to be broken—the beliefs, practices, and assumptions we need to challenge. They cover the gamut, from the societal to the social, from the personal to business—all enveloped in the belief that we are created equal and that our spiritual being cannot be separated from any aspect of our life at any time. Strikethroughs indicate these are *not* rules to follow.

1. ~~The American Dream is for all.~~ The pursuit of the American Dream is a false pursuit to assert on the poor of our society. In the Forgotten America, that of the poor and disenfranchised, they have almost no chance in a merit-based system, and there is no level playing field. They have so many cultural and societal barriers that prevent them from even being able to play the game.

2. ~~Meritocracy works for everybody.~~ This concept of standing with everyone and, in particular, the most despised, stands in stark contrast to how the rest of the world believes and values a merit-based system—a system of measuring up, the "old-fashioned work ethic." The disenfranchised cannot "bootstrap" themselves up—they have no bootstraps to begin with!

3. ~~You just need to work hard to get ahead.~~ The central theme of "hard work and dedication to an endeavor" in the American Dream narrative is an overemphasized value when the people from the Privileged America look at those from the Forgotten America and can't figure out why they are having difficulty. The thinking goes so far as to accuse people of being lazy, not caring, or being good-for-nothings. Educator Paulo Freire's position is that the elite or privileged feel entitled to their position. The oppressor is angered by what he sees as the oppressed's "ingratitude" for the "generosity" shown to them.

4. ~~It's possible to measure people's worth.~~ Finding one's worth is not a metric—there is no way to calculate that. To discover the God-given goodness of people—there is no way to measure that. Specifically, someone doesn't transform their life "better or sooner" than someone else.

5. ~~Society has solved the problem of racism.~~ Our only chance at dismantling racial injustice is to be more curious about how it still exists today than to be worried about our comfort should we discover how we may have contributed to it. To give ourselves a "free pass" on recrimination is to absentmindedly foster racism. Once awareness sets in, we must develop action to change the dynamic.

6. ~~I'm not racist, so it's other people who need to change.~~ Without a doubt racism exists, even in those of us who do not intend to act out of bias and prejudice; we are all part of a system that fosters racism. The question is, what are we as members of society to do about it? What are our roles? How do we create systematic change? Do we need to change the structure of our society or just work to change our attitudes? Make reforms within your organization and support societal policies that do the same.

7. ~~The world is all about "us" and "them."~~ It's harder to demonize someone you know—relationship counteracts tribalism and judgmentalism. Get to know your coworkers. Seek to understand the lived experiences and histories of those who come from a culture different from your own. Don't demonize anyone.

8. ~~I'm at the top of my profession, so I know what to do.~~ Being well trained for the business world doesn't mean all that much when leading the way forward in other arenas—we need to know our limits. Be open to knowing that you need to learn new things.

9. ~~Jump into action.~~ Father Greg's early advice of listening, learning, and becoming part of the community was good advice for me, as it made me pause and slow down. Our mission is strong. Our people know how to get gang members out of gang life, so don't come in here as a volunteer to "fix" us. Rather, come in and be part of our family and look to support and help.

10. ~~You can think about faith later.~~ Homeboy helped me discover more about faith in general and about my faith in particular. What is there for you to discover about your faith? We must do our own inner work before we can help others with a truly generous and giving heart, otherwise it's about us "saving others."

11. ~~Make ambition a priority and climb that ladder.~~ This individualistic mentality does nothing more than separate us from our true selves and from those around us. It is pouring empty into empty. When the ego falls into scarcity, it is unable to harness all that is available to us when we pour generously into each other. The abundance we all receive as a result of this shift in mindset is exponentially greater—in every dimension—than that which we could achieve on our own.

12. ~~In this world there are winners and losers.~~ Let's dare to think always in terms of win-win. One person having success does not mean that success is taken from someone else. Generosity and gratitude need to be cultivated and put into action so that everyone is able to succeed. This can happen for all, not just for those who work in an organization like Homeboy. You can shift your mindset even in large bureaucratic organizations. It's about an individual mindset that spreads into a collective mindset.

13. ~~Good logic always leads to good business.~~ Up until this point in my life, logic had served me well—or so it seemed. But the rules of logic often inhibit us from taking leaps of faith into uncharted territories, where unimaginable gifts await.

14. ~~We should always strive for certainty.~~ I broke my rule of certainty and instead used the rule of faith that we would have a normal fundraising fall—that the money would be replenished. Certainty will blind you to your own biases and conclusions. We need to be comfortable managing in times of uncertainty, particularly in human-services organizations.

15. ~~Responsibility is a burden.~~ In loving God, burdens turn into joys. Everyone should pursue joy. In that pursuit, I found my path forward. The stressors of the responsibility I once felt are now secondary to the times where I found joy. Joy is a powerful state. Finding joy takes time, contemplation, and openness. Once there, everything else in life just falls into place.

16. ~~Keep professional life separate from personal life.~~ Following your spiritual path does not move you away from life as you know it—it only enhances the life you have. This work is so very important if you want to engage fully in the life of following God or your higher power as you know it. This is not something you learn at a management seminar, nor is it a requirement to advance up the career ladder—but without it, life will not be full and joyous.

17. ~~Stick with the status quo or proven concepts.~~ Break the rules of conventional wisdom that have become cemented in our collective thinking. Particularly those taught in business school, such as the number one golden rule of business—to "maximize shareholder value." If you ever find yourself thinking, "There's gotta be a better way," then there probably is.

18. ~~Show people the error of their ways.~~ It took me a while to learn not to judge people who got into awful situations. I've learned to suppress that urge and just help the person who is in front of me today who has tragically tough choices to make. There's no need to always point out the mistakes of others.

19. ~~"They should have known better."~~ Maybe they should have known better, but in many situations, you and I should have known better too. The difference is that people on the margins have no cushion for mistakes, and they cannot recover as easily as someone who has resources and a support network. Many actions of people who are poor are shaped by shame and other factors. Don't judge people, even when their actions are clearly wrong. You most certainly will misread the situation. Find out what the root causes of those actions are.

20. ~~Accountability is permanent.~~ God is too busy loving us to be judging us. There is no such thing as an evil person, and no one should ever be defined by the worst thing they have ever done.

21. ~~Some people are just evil.~~ People are not evil; they are made in God's image and always carry good. Everyone deserves a chance to overcome the violence of their past and to heal so that the cycle of violence has a chance of being broken. If we discount someone as evil, we feel no responsibility to help them. It's countercultural to stick with a person regardless of what he or she has done.

22. ~~The "simple life" is impossible.~~ Our people have that natural ability to live life so generously. Our homies live simply, with no pretenses, and they're here to help other people. I think they are just more spacious with their generosity, and in this way, I feel they are more in God's light. Since God gives with abundance, shouldn't we all?

23. ~~Grace is rare, an exception to the rule.~~ People who work with homies and other outcasts of society discover just how much grace is at work—and how often. What choices am I making in my personal life, within my personal relationships, to be available for moments of grace? To be more generous and grateful? Grace is there and available—it happens to us through the practice of generosity and gratitude.

24. ~~Every person is responsible for himself or herself.~~ Each and every person who is looking to be in our program has the desire to "do good," "to be better," "to be the person they are meant to be." The struggle is that they don't know how to make this transition on their own and the structural barriers that exist are insurmountable for most, regardless of how hard they work. What can we do in our organizations to facilitate transitions for those who are struggling?

25. ~~So-called white privilege does not exist.~~ Recognize that some of us do have privilege and some of us don't. We must work to live in exquisite mutuality. We must work to ensure everyone has a fair chance to live a healthy, happy, and dignified life. Those of us with privilege can use our resources at the margin of society to unite the margin with the rest of society.

26. ~~Money won't solve your problems.~~ We at Homeboy, I think, do a phenomenal job of helping people navigate tough transitions as they move through their recovery pathways. And money does make a huge difference in making these transitions happen. Money does help solve problems for people who are in need of life's basics, such as food, shelter, medical care, and employment opportunities.

27. ~~A business is an entity unto itself.~~ Business is not insulated from its surroundings. All businesses are local businesses. Being a stakeholder in the betterment of the community not only helps local businesses but also, by extension, lifts up everyone in the community.

28. ~~The boss is always right and deserves your respect.~~ Step back when you find yourself needing to be right or requiring absolute respect. There is always something else behind "insubordination"—the stresses of life catch up to many people and happen to us all. To change one's life is hard work, and there's dignity in this hard work. It is in this hard work where, paradoxically, profound healing begins. So let us all not be angry and judgmental when we feel threatened by a slight workplace dis. Let us view it as a chance to be humble and to acknowledge someone else's pain.

29. ~~Everyone already knows how to work.~~ Let's not think everybody understands well all workplace etiquette. If you didn't grow up in a loving family where many of these norms were taught, it would be hard for you to figure it out by yourself.

30. ~~In the workplace, tenderness is a sign of weakness.~~ Tenderness is a sign of strength, not weakness. I'm thankful that my misunderstanding and cluelessness were met with patience and tenderness from Father Greg and the homies. Can you imagine how this type of tenderness and understanding might transform workplaces on the "outside"? Tenderness and compassion need to be given in all facets of our life, not just in our home life where it's easiest to give.

31. ~~The boss creates the culture for the team.~~ The characteristics of an organization's leadership can have an enduring effect on culture long after the leaders are gone—for better or for worse. The gift of displaying tenderness, compassion, and patience in the workplace is the understanding that it sets the tone for the organization's collective character. It is this *collective* character that informs core values, policies, rituals, and other culture-related practices that endure. The goal is to understand that the collective character is more powerful than the individual ego.

32. ~~Be stoic and aloof in the workplace to avoid lawsuits.~~ If your employees feel valued, even loved, conflicts will be easier to resolve. Practice humor, laughter, and hugs in the workplace. This does not mean the type of humor that cleverly disguises sarcasm—remarks that feel like little daggers and mock or show contempt for others—or the type of hugs that are creepy. Lean into the laughter so you can learn not to take yourself too seriously. Special note to corporate attorneys and human resource professionals: hugs work and make a difference. They allow for a generous giving of oneself.

33. ~~The organization should come before the employees.~~ The employees *are* the organization, and we should never lose sight of the individual. Do what is best for the individual in front of you—which may not always be what is best for the organization. As you follow the core values of an organization, you may notice that they don't necessarily line up with your personal core values at times—be aware of the difference. Treat people as individuals, not as a mass.

34. ~~Proven expertise should come before diversity.~~ Collectively, as we in society aim to employ the "unemployable," we need to cultivate managers who are strong in both functional expertise and in facilitating equitable team diversity, particularly as more people from different cultures and lived experiences—other than our own—come on board.

35. ~~Make savings a top priority.~~ To Father Greg's point, why have a rainy-day fund when we have torrential rainstorms every day? The need is to invest now. Why hoard assets? I've met a few very special people who make the commitment to ensure their money is used up within their lifetimes. To those folks, I salute you in the highest regard, for you have certainly figured out the specialness of generosity.

36. ~~Long-term stability is paramount.~~ In human-services organizations, the thinking shouldn't be to cut expenses, which has the tradeoff of helping fewer people—particularly when times get tough. The priority should be to raise more money to help more people. Father Greg's instinct isn't to worry about the future of "the organization" but rather, to do all we can to help the people standing in front of us today. This perspective often rows in the opposite direction of what the board will want. They want stability, longevity, and sustainability. This tension is natural, but in helping the poor, we can "save" our way to helping more people. We must avoid overcaution and do everything possible to raise funds now.

37. ~~Advancement systems should be color-blind and color-neutral.~~ For corporate America to unlock the potential of a workforce that has been underemployed and under-utilized, it must put effort into reversing racial inequities. Think about leadership- and people-development efforts differently. Develop policies and practices that go to great lengths to remove unconscious bias and intentionally create access to opportunities for people of color. You will need to overinvest time and energy to do this, including asking people of color within your organization for insight on critical points of intervention. Think differently about how to successfully make this happen.

38. ~~Businesses should steer clear of the race issue.~~ In many organizations, open discussions about race issues have been discouraged to avoid conflict. But silence does not lead to solutions. We must first contemplate our own actions and attitudes, then act to work from within the structures of our organizations to enable these discussions to occur. This is a tall order, particularly for someone who works in a large corporation. As with most things, large shifts in direction and policies need to come from the top leadership team in collaboration with those they wish to create equity for. Organizations that have developed a learning culture will be the first ones able to make the shift.

39. ~~Success is about education and seniority.~~ Lived experience and histories are important when the work is focused on joining the Two Americas. While this concept seems exactly right for human-service agencies, it also works for all organizations that value having a diverse workforce. To accomplish this, you need to get rid of the structures currently in place for advancement. Real-life experience and workplace experience need to be valued more than educational attainment and seniority. This change needs to be initiated from the top, triggering the necessary and *intentional* shift in organizational culture and mindset.

40. ~~A promotion should always be earned.~~ The business world usually says to someone looking for a promotion, "Before you get the promotion you need to take on those responsibilities and demonstrate that you can do the job." People understand this dynamic and willingly put forth the effort, for they trust that they will get the promotion in a merit-based environment. We know this doesn't always play out on the "outside," and it certainly doesn't work in the Homeboy world. Because of their bad experiences, some people will not take on more work or responsibility unless they receive the promotion/raise up front. They have learned that for people like them, you can't expect that hard work will lead to real payoff. They are system-impacted: they've had a lot of experiences of being lied to, talked down to, and offered false promises and commitments by bureaucracy and management teams led by authority figures (mostly white guys), who never really followed through on anything for them to make their lives better.

41. ~~It's easier to hire for management skill sets than to develop them.~~ The effort to develop the management team that is partially composed of leaders with lived experiences requires time, money, and most important, a mindset the whole organization needs to take on. It is the blending of the talent of those from the Two Americas that is the greatest struggle. When it works, you get a beautiful mix of many different talents with everyone leaning in on their strengths to accomplish the mission.

42. ~~Give the exact same support to everyone.~~ To truly provide leadership opportunities for people with lived experiences, we need to overinvest in them and set them up in positions that play to their strengths—which may require short-term clerical or administrative support. Don't be worried about some people getting more help than others in developing your next generation of leaders. As you're raising the skill sets of people, be flexible and generous in providing the additional support they need on an individual level.

43. ~~If I can do it, anyone can.~~ The success of someone like me, who had support and resources along the way, is not proof that anyone from any background can start at the very bottom and work their way up. As the country reckons with how best to improve racial equity, I believe a main factor will be how to bring more people along—out of poverty—and into quality jobs that provide for growth up the economic ladder. What needs to clearly be said is it's not good enough to just provide entry level—usually minimum wage—positions. We need to provide jobs that lead to something more substantive and equitable. To do so will mean an overinvestment in terms of access to continuing resources while people are working. A very proactive approach is to create opportunities for guidance, mentorship, and coaching.

44. ~~Merit-driven culture is good for everybody.~~ Creating a workplace culture where one can thrive is the goal. As Father Greg says, "Achievements are a by-product of thriving." At Homeboy our efforts are focused on providing an atmosphere where people flourish and blossom so that they find their own worth. The key is not measuring merit but facilitating joy in the workplace. This opens the door to experiencing deep moments of grace, individually and collectively. Imagine a society that collectively pursues and reaches the goal of having thriving workplaces. This is when we as a society can do away with meritocracy and just celebrate achievements.

45. ~~You can't trust people who have felonies to be good employees.~~ The Homeboy workforce in our social enterprises are just as valuable and competent as workforces in corporate America. The business managers in our social enterprises, who were once clients, are just as talented and trustworthy (if not more) as the managers who worked for me in my big corporation. Hire and invest in people who have done their time and paid their debt to society.

46. ~~Employees are interchangeable and dispensable.~~ The $6MDM challenge I've always faced is the tension between how to build a great company for the shareholders and its employees—at the same time. The investment world values top talent—the $6MDM-type skill set—but doesn't value frontline employees and is allergic to the notion of providing long-term employment. This comes from a scarcity mindset—get in and get the return, then get out before the opportunity is gone. The way forward is to build businesses for the long-term. Long-term employability, long-term profitability, long-term impact.

47. ~~Make the numbers and protect the organization.~~ Homeboy "reverse cherry-picks"—that is, we take the applicants who most need to work in our organization. We help those who ask us for help, without worrying about whether they will make our numbers look good or not. Manage for the mission, not for the numbers. In the long-term, this strategy will take care of the numbers. Protecting the organization's reputation at the expense of those who need help the most is an injustice. Stand for all people, no matter what.

48. ~~Invest capital only in "tried and true" business models.~~ To make true progress in our society, investment capital needs to be deployed in different and innovative ways. Baking more bread to hire more homies means it's up to us to create businesses that maximize the number of good, quality jobs. Lean into the collective intelligence and creativity of your workforce for business innovations—then let them run with it. Invest into "baking more bread" to make a return on social value as the priority. Equitable financial returns are the goal.

49. ~~Maximize shareholder value.~~ Economic Equality Capitalism done the Homeboy way is as simple as investing in businesses that provide economic opportunities to people who have not been given a fair shot before. This investment is not hard to make—it just takes the willingness to not fall into the trap of "maximizing shareholder value," which generally requires either producing high yields or a turnaround. The mindset needs to be financial returns *and* employment stability.

50. ~~I take care of me; you take care of you.~~ As Archbishop Desmond Tutu said, "Ultimately, our greatest joy is when we seek to do good for others." Our goal as leaders is to facilitate organizational joy as we, on an individual level, move ourselves to joy—a joy that is pure, a joy that is openhearted, and a joy that is humble.

51. ~~I learned about God when I was young.~~ Seek to understand God better. Specifically for me, I came to realize that my own spirituality was a bit shallow. I had to find an understanding that was more substantive, more grounding. I had to mature a lot more in my spiritual growth, in my understanding of God and how to live—and lead—in a faith-based way that is inclusive of all.

52. ~~My job defines me.~~ The point for me is that without the benefit of what I've learned so far on my journey, my life would be out of balance. I would constantly be stressed about work struggles, and I would make these "problems" front and center all the time in my life. These struggles would define who I am, how I view others. A life defined by a workplace would not only be frustrating but would also be dark.

53. ~~I have arrived.~~ Here I am today, having traveled far along my spiritual path compared with where I started, but not very far in the bigger picture. Each of us always has more to learn. It's best not to think in terms of a final destination but of continually going deeper and being more open to God every day, using God-given gifts to help others, and doing our work with grace and love.

54. ~~My gifts are not the help-people type.~~ We need to pay attention to the gifts we have and pray and meditate on what God would want us to do with those gifts. There is not you and a spiritual you; there is just you. And the unique gifts you have will be used, eventually, to help the world as God desires.

55. ~~God does not really accept me.~~ Discover faith at a "gut and heart" level. As Richard Rohr writes in his book *The Universal Christ*, "Faith at its essential core is *accepting that you are accepted*."[37] What Homeboy has shown me is that I'm accepted by God—always, and no matter what. So are you.

---

37. Richard Rohr, *The Universal Christ: How a Forgotten Reality Can Change Everything We See, Hope For, and Believe* (New York: Convergent Books/Penguin Random House, 2019), 29, italics in the original.

ACKNOWLEDGMENTS

Dorothy Day said, "Sow kindness and you will reap kindness—sow love and you will reap love." This effort of writing about Homeboy could not have been accomplished without the many people who have sowed kindness and love in me throughout my life. I thank you all. Particularly I thank Father Greg and the homies for allowing me to be part of the community and who have taught me so much.

This writing effort could not have been accomplished without my friend Jodie Masters-Gonzales, who spent countless hours with me, shaping the concepts and the narrative of this story. Her passion and steadfastness in seeking to illuminate the lessons of Homeboy were incomparable.

I thank the good folks at Loyola Press who took a chance on a first-time writer and worked to make the book and message better. Vinita Wright's edits and insightful suggestions belied a deep knowledge of the issues Homeboy faced, which was very instrumental to bringing the story together.

To the leadership team at Homeboy. While some are named in this book, many are not; either way, Homeboy would not exist without these talented and dedicated individuals. Often and rightly so, we prioritize the trainee (client) at Homeboy. We celebrate their transformation, the heroic changing of their life, the subtle shifts in their mindset. With this, what gets lost is the humble work of the senior team and their quiet attention to mission. My heart is full of gratitude for all of them. I also thank this team for sticking with me and Homeboy while we went through the financial ups and downs of being a "spend every penny" human-services organization.

I want to thank the many Homeboy board members (current and previous) who have given generously of their time and who have helped guide the organization along with a generous heart. In particular, I want to thank our Board Chair, Pernille Lopez, who has been a good advisor to me and who has imparted quiet wisdom to the organization with a steady hand.

I want to thank again and again the many volunteers and donors of Homeboy; many I've developed good friendships with. Homeboy would not be the organization it is today without their steadfast support.

I want to thank the many advisors and mentors I had in my career. In particular, I want to thank Elmer Orloff, whose sage advice was always on the mark. Additionally, I want to thank all the men and women who have worked with me over the many years—your support and friendship have been special.

I've come to appreciate the value of balance in life, and I want to thank my many friends who have always been there for me. For all the members of our HHF trail hiking club, who weekly have helped keep me fit and always were there as a sounding board for me as we hiked down the mountain. Likewise, I very much appreciate the efforts of Jenna, who consistently encouraged me to keep setting goals to keep me whole, mentally and physically.

I also thank Gordon Bennett and Randall Roche, who have been my spiritual advisors and who patiently and gracefully led me to a deeper understanding of God.

As I look at my extended family, I am grateful for all the support I've received from all the Vozzos and Bruckers. The values I learned from all of them and the generations before them have formed and impacted my life.

To my sons, Louis and Paul. I'm proud of the fine men you are, and my heart bursts with love for each of you.

To my wife, Lindy. We have been together since we were eighteen years old, and you have always been there to support me—through all the phases of our life—and you have always believed in me. My love for you is everlasting and complete. You are my soulmate forever.

ABOUT THE AUTHOR

For much of his career, Thomas Vozzo was a global business executive with a proven track record, leading highly successful businesses in the service, retail, and distribution industries. He is well regarded for growing businesses and is known for strong execution skills, constantly exceeding earnings targets, even during challenging economic times. His last corporate role was as CEO of the $1.8 billion ARAMARK Uniform and Career Apparel Group.

His definition of transformation changed dramatically with his introduction to Father Greg Boyle, the founder of Homeboy Industries. As he began working at the nonprofit organization, Vozzo himself noted, "The blind spot I had is typical for so many of us. Through no fault of our own, by just being in the mainstream of society, we stay isolated from those most unlike ourselves and outside our station in life."

In 2012, Vozzo started serving as the first CEO of Homeboy Industries, the largest and most successful gang rehabilitation and re-entry program in the world. Vozzo, as a non-paid employee, has led the organization, bringing his business expertise and vision to implement a strategic and mission-driven plan, resulting in a near tripling of the size of the organization and increasing its impact. In helping Homeboy Industries thrive over the past several years, Vozzo says he has "gained knowledge and insight about my own spirituality and the plight of the underserved and marginalized in our society."

In 2020 Homeboy was awarded the prestigious Conrad N. Hilton Humanitarian Prize for its humanitarian impact. Vozzo has also launched a $15 million Homeboy Ventures and Jobs Fund, which will provide likeminded people a way to invest in businesses that produce quality jobs that lead to real economic impact for our society.

It is Vozzo's goal to work himself out of his current CEO role and get out of the way—to make room for the homeboys and homegirls to run Homeboy. He is confident they will lead the organization into a bright future.